There's a Chef in your Freezer

There's a Chef in your Freezer

fast, fabulous, delicious Mediterranean-inspired
recipes your family, friends, and you will love

by Richard Azzolini

There's a Chef in your Freezer
Copyright © 2001 Richard Azzolini
All rights reserved

Universal Publishers / uPUBLISH.com
2002 • USA

ISBN: 1-58112-654-9

www.upublish.com/books/azzolini.htm

This book is dedicated to my three muses—

Vera Azzolini

Mary Bavaro

Dolores Bavaro Azzolini

... three wonderful women who allowed a young boy to observe,
stir, and taste as they worked their kitchen magic.

Thank you... I loved you all so much.

Acknowledgments

First and foremost I want to thank Henry Rabinowitz, who offered unending support, keen editing, and much encouragement throughout the writing and publishing process. A finer person and a better partner you could not find. Thank you!

Rebecca Rabinowitz is responsible for the book's fab layout. Her skill, artistic eye, and advice were a tremendous asset. Hilary Sweeney assisted Rebecca with the layout. Thank you!

John Martin shot the cover photographs with Rebecca Rabinowitz acting as the stylist. (Do I look fabulous or what!) Rebecca also designed the cover. Thank you!

Ivy Eisenberg helped with the book editing. Thank you!

Carole Eiserloh helped tremendously by reading the manuscript. Carole offered some great ideas, which I have included in the text. Thank you!

Bonnie and Richard Azzolini, Kerry Weisel, Justine and Bob Lobe, Esther Rubin, Donna Brorby, Andrea Brown, Francis von Lukanovic, Pearl Rabinowitz, Mordechai Rabinowitz, Jean Hamerman, Stephen Errante, Michelle Gross and Andy Zaff, Lothar Eiserloh, Tom and Ellen Azzolini, John and Maryann Azzolini, Mary and Alan Ledesky are among the friends and family who offered support and ideas throughout the process of this book's creation. Thank you!

Table of Contents

Contents

Contents

Introduction

In a perfect world everyone would have as much time as they wanted to prepare delicious meals for themselves and their loved ones. Unfortunately, most people today find it difficult to take the time to prepare meals starting from scratch. After a long day of work who feels like coming home and roasting a bunch of peppers or making a batch of fresh tomato sauce? But there is another approach....

If you are willing to do some preparation when the time is more convenient, you can have many delicious edible building blocks at your fingertips that you can quickly assemble into a superb meal. I call these building blocks "sunshine in the freezer." What are they? Blanched and peeled tomatoes, roasted peppers, sautéed wild mushrooms, meltingly soft leeks and onions, and lots of roasted garlic, purée of squash, aromatic chicken stock, purée of basil, and a rosemary and thyme marinade—all ingredients that freeze well and will facilitate your turning a steaming bowl of soup, some pasta, a chicken breast, or a nice salmon filet into a feast in short order.

I wrote this book for people who enjoy good simple food with a Mediterranean accent. The first part of the book focuses on how to prepare the edible building blocks you will need to create the recipes in the second part of the book. Every restaurant kitchen has its own *mise en place,* the chef's version of edible building blocks. This book will show you how to create a similar set of building blocks for your home kitchen. The building blocks can be used the next day, the next week, or kept in the freezer to be pulled out at a moment's notice from your frozen pantry. Unlike raw ingredients, the building blocks freeze beautifully, without losing their texture, flavor, or wholesomeness. The recipes in the second part of this book are designed to allow you to create delicious meals when time is at a premium.

While you can make building blocks at any time of year, during the late summer and fall, when produce is at its peak of ripeness and flavor, and at its lowest price, take advantage! Become a gourmand squirrel and stock up to make the building blocks for the dreary winter ahead.

When preparing the building blocks, I encourage you to invite some fellow food lovers and make it a party. Why not buy a whole case of red peppers, shiitake mushrooms, golden onions, or a pile of chicken bones, and process them together to the accompaniment of a good glass of wine and your favorite music? Then, you can divide up the resulting building blocks by weight or volume—everyone gets to take home their share. Another wonderful advantage of group cooking is wholesale buying. When you can buy produce by the case you will realize substantial savings.

You can drink, dish and groove while you prepare the ingredients for great meals to come. Such a party is like an updated quilting bee, except that instead of coming together to make a quilt from squares of material, you are creating edible building blocks. What a great way to spend a rainy afternoon—creating your own freezer-full of sunshine.

Richard Azzolini

Visit my web site at www.chefaz.com

Contact Richard Azzolini to receive the Chef AZ Newsletter which will feature new recipes and other items of culinary interest.

Want a signed copy of this book? I will send you a signed dedication sticker you can place in the book. Just contact me.

Any comments, thoughts, and questions welcome. Wishing you many happy hours in the kitchen,

Richard Azzolini
'le chef'

© New York, 2001

Email: Chefaz@aol.com   *Mention 'book' in subject so I'll know it's not spam.*
Snail mail: Richard Azzolini, Cathedral Station, P.O. Box 1162, NY NY 10025

Building Blocks

Tomatoes

Succulent love apples, ripe, juicy tomatoes are among the kitchen's greatest treasures. Late summer and early autumn, when tomatoes are vine ripe, inexpensive, and bursting with flavor, is the best time to put up a large batch to use later when the summer sun fades.

Our tomato preparations will use beefsteak or any full-size tomatoes and plum or Roma tomatoes. The riper you can find them the better. In fact, you can often buy over-ripe tomatoes at a good discount from farm-stands and produce markets. Ask your greengrocer to save you the softies—they are culinary gold!

If the tomatoes need a little extra ripening, try this trick: put them in a brown paper bag with a banana, seal the bag, and put it in a cool place for a day or two. The ethyline gas the banana releases will ripen the tomatoes.

Concasse Tomatoes and Tomato Nectar

Beefsteak Tomatoes—concasse

You will need to process the tomatoes that you've brought home or grown before you can use them in many wonderful dishes. There are four steps; I recommend you process all the tomatoes through each step before you go on to the next step. The result of this process is known as concasse tomatoes.

1. Wash all the tomatoes in a large bowl of cool water with a drop of soap like Dr. Bronner's to remove any dirt. Rinse the tomatoes. Cut out the core and the stem spot—the spot where the tomato was attached to the stem—of each beefsteak tomato. There is a small tool called a *tomato shark*—it looks like a serrated mini melon baller—that makes this a one-second task.

2. Next, we want to remove the skins. The easiest way to do this is to drop the tomatoes into boiling water for a quick dip to loosen the skin. How long to dip is the question. The riper the tomato, the shorter the time necessary. The goal is to blanch just until the skin can be easily removed. Use one tomato to test the time needed: Take one tomato and drop it into the water; remove it after 30 seconds, and drop it into a pan of cold water. Now take a paring knife and see if the skin comes off easily. If not, return the test tomato to the boiling water for another dip and retest. Once you have determined the approximate time, you can process several tomatoes at once. Be careful not to overcook, or the tomatoes will become mushy and more difficult to work with. For best results, blanch as quickly as possible. Once you have blanched all the tomatoes, pull off the skins with a sharp paring knife. Save the skin—it's full of flavor. We will use it later.

3. Cut the tomatoes in half. It's important to make the cut in the right direction so you can squeeze the most out of the tomatoes. If you think of the stem end as the north pole and the opposite end as the south pole, then make the cut through the "equator." Now, gently squeeze out the seeds. The easiest way to do this is to grasp the tomato-half in the palm of your hand, cut-side facing out, held perpendicular to the counter and over a bowl. Squeeze the tomato-half gently, and use the fingers of your other

11

hand to to help dislodge the seeds and pulp so they fall into the bowl. If you find the tomato juice irritating to your skin, I suggest you use disposable vinyl or latex gloves, available at a drugstore.

The goal here is to remove as many of the seeds as possible. Seeds get hard when cooked and become slightly bitter. Remember, the Duchess of Windsor fired her chef when she found a seed in her tomato bisque. (I'm not suggesting you must remove every last seed but let the Duchess be your inspiration!) Save all the seeds and juice that you remove. You will use them to make tomato nectar.

4. The tomatoes are now ready to be used in recipes. They can be used whole or chopped into ½ inch cubes.

This process results in a very refined tomato product. Making a tomato purée is actually simpler—we'll explain how at the end of this chapter.

But first let's not ignore the tomato seeds, skins and juice that we've set aside in preparing the concasse. They are full of flavor and will yield a wonderful tomato nectar.

Preparing tomato nectar

1. In a food processor or blender put all the skin, juice, and seeds. Process until liquified.

2. Pass the resulting liquid through a fine sieve or strainer. The best strainer for this purpose is called a *chinoise*. A chinoise is a conical strainer with a very fine mesh. I have found that the easiest way to extract the juice is to press and push down and against the side of the strainer with your fingers or a rubber spatula. The strainer should be fine enough to keep out the seeds—remember, the Duchess is watching!

3. To concentrate the flavor, bring the liquid to a boil. Lower the heat to a strong simmer and reduce by half, until it has the consistency of canned tomato juice (of course it will taste much better!)

4. Once the juice is sufficiently reduced, strain it.

5. The tomato nectar is now ready to use. If you like, you can continue to cook it. Eventually, it will become sauce-like in consistency and concentrated in flavor.

Variations

To make the tomato nectar even more interesting, you can add some of these flavor enhancers: onion, leek greens, Italian parsley stalks, garlic, roasted garlic skins (see p. 19), carrots, celery, and herbs such as thyme, rosemary, oregano, or bay leaf. The goal is to add a subtle flavoring, so don't go overboard. For each quart of juice, add at least 1 cup of rough-chopped vegetables. A few sprigs of fresh herbs will be fine.

This will produce a very delicious nectar which can be used as a drink (you never had a Bloody Mary so good), a poaching liquid for fish or chicken, a base for soup, or a "stock" for a great tomato risotto.

Oven Roasted Tomatoes and Tomato Purée

Plum tomatoes can be prepared using the concasse method above, but I find it simpler to oven roast them. Oven roasting makes for a more "rustic tomato," but it is much easier to do. Good news for those of you who were anticipating nightmares from peeling all those tomatoes! Here are the steps:

Oven Roasted Plum Tomatoes

1. Wash the plum tomatoes thoroughly, drain them in a colander, and split them in half down the length of the tomato.

2. Scoop out the seeds and set aside. A melon baller makes this quick work. You can process the seeds the same way as for beef-steak tomato seeds (see above).

3. Lay the tomatoes in a baking dish which has been very lightly brushed with olive oil or sprayed with a non-stick olive oil spray. It's OK if the tomatoes overlap, but don't pile them up; it's better to use more pans. Non-stick pans work well for this purpose. Drizzle the tomatoes with a little olive oil and sprinkle lightly with sea salt and fresh-ground black pepper. (The olive oil can be omitted if you desire a fat-free purée, but the purée will not taste as good!)

4. Roast in a 350° oven until soft. This should take about one hour. Remove them from the oven.

   The tomatoes are now ready to use. They can be used whole, diced, or processed into a smooth purée. One advantage of puréeing is that the skins will be pulverized and become part of the smooth sauce. This purée can be enhanced to make sauces and soups. I find a blender is indispensable in creating the tomato purée. Just add the following step to the previous ones:

Plum tomato purée

5. Allow the tomatoes to cool slightly. Fill the blender jar, but be careful not to over-fill it. Keep the lid slightly ajar when you turn on the blender to avoid a steam build-up, which can result in a spattered mess. (This rule applies whenever you are using a blender with warm ingredients.) It is a good idea to start the blender on a slow speed, then to finish on the highest speed.

You will be amazed at the result. The skins vanish into the purée. A food processor would chop up the tomatoes, but would leave bits of the skin recognizable—yuk! The blender totally pulverizes the skins. They become part of the smooth purée without the unpleasant texture tomato skins would otherwise impart. This purée will find uses in the chapters on sauces, soups, and salad dressings.

Oven-dried plum tomatoes

Follow the directions for the oven-roasted plum tomatoes through step 3. Roast the tomatoes in a 250° oven for 5 to 6 hours, until the tomatoes have shrunk by half their size. This will result in the tomatoes having a very intense flavor. They can be processed into a thick paste via the blender method, or used chopped or whole.

Oven-roasted Beefsteak Tomatoes

1. Wash and seed the tomatoes as discussed in the concasse preparation section above (p.11, steps 1 and 3) but omit the blanching (step 2).

2. Place the tomatoes cut side up into a baking dish prepared as for plum tomatoes. You can squeeze them in as tightly as you like but do not overlap them.

3. Drizzle with a little olive oil and sprinkle with sea salt and freshly ground black pepper.

4. Roast in a 350° oven until soft and lightly colored, approximately 60-75 minutes.

5. Remove from the oven. Unlike plum tomatoes, beefsteaks will release a lot of liquid during the cooking process.

6. Place the tomatoes in a colander and let the juices drain into a bowl. Save every drop! The juice can be processed as we did for the tomato nectar above (p.12), except for one difference. The olive oil will drain off with the liquid. I suggest you skim it off the surface and add it to the tomatoes.

7. There are two ways to process the tomatoes. The skins will slip off easily now. You can simply slip off the skins and leave the tomatoes whole, or process them in a blender as you would the plum tomatoes (p.14).

Given all the methods discussed in this chapter to prepare tomato building blocks, which method should you employ? The answer depends on how much effort you are willing to put in, and on the uses you will make of these building blocks. For soups and sauces the oven roasted purée works excellently. The concasse tomatoes are great for garnishes in salads and soups, and for adding color and flavor to our quick-sauté recipes.

Garlic

The smell of cooking garlic wafting through the air promises wonderful tastes to follow. Garlic adds its special magic to many savory dishes from simple pasta with garlic and olive oil to rich and creamy purée of garlic soup.(p.81) Marry garlic with tomatoes and you have a match made in heaven. Garlic is available year round, but if you are very lucky you may find new garlic—that is—garlic that has not been cured by drying. One September during a food mad trip to Paris, we found new garlic in the outdoor markets. It had a sweet, mild flavor. We sautéed mounds of wild mushrooms with the garlic and oven roasted many heads. It was a dream to eat. So if you can find it, use the new garlic. If not, look for plump cloves with tight outer skin, firm to the touch. Dull-looking cloves with loose papery skins or any that are soft to the touch or sprouting should be avoided.

For the recipes in this book we will be using cooked garlic. Cooking gives garlic a softer flavor. I love garlic and eat huge amounts of it, but I find raw garlic gives me heartburn. I know I'm not the only one who reacts this way, so I have adapted some traditional recipes using cooked garlic in place of raw. The recipes are still quite delicious.

My favorite way to prepare garlic as a building block is oven roasting.

Preparing Garlic by Oven-Roasting

It is very easy to roast garlic. Here are two methods, the whole-head roasting method, and the individual cloves roasting method.

Whole-head roasting method

1. Cut off the top ½ inch of the crown of the garlic head, saving the top. Place the garlic head root-side-down on a sheet of foil that has been lightly coated with olive oil or sprayed with a non-stick spray. Drizzle a little olive oil and grind some fresh black pepper over the cut. (Be sure to use fresh ground pepper only; pre-ground pepper is a very poor substitute.) Replace the crown. Now bring up both sides of the foil and fold over to make a tent. Add a teaspoon of water for each head. Fold up both ends of the foil to seal the package.

2. Roast in a 350° oven for 45 minutes until the side of the head yields when squeezed. You can roast several heads at a time. Be careful not to overbake, or the garlic could dry out and become bitter. You are allowed to "peek" while the garlic is roasting, but beware of escaping steam from the foil envelope, and be sure to carefully reseal the envelope. After a few times, you'll get a sense of how the garlic feels through the foil when it is ready.

If you want to make super roast garlic, all you have to do is add some fresh herbs to the package. Add any combination of the following herbs, laying them across the cut top of the garlic head—just a sprig or two is enough: thyme (a must!), rosemary (wonderful), bay leaf (adds depth, but use a piece of a leaf, not a whole one), oregano (Mama mia!), or sage (just a leaf will do). The herbs will add their perfume to the garlic, and the result will be heavenly.

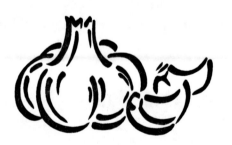

Individual Cloves roasting method

Separate the garlic into cloves, place them on a sheet of foil, prepared as for the whole-head method. Lay down a single layer of garlic cloves, loosely touching. Sprinkle the fresh herbs over them, and then lay down a second layer of garlic cloves over the herbs. Drizzle with a little olive oil, add 1 teaspoon of water for each head, and seal up the foil into a closed packet. Roast about 30 minutes at 350° until the cloves are soft to the touch. Be careful not to overbake.

Storing the Prepared Garlic

Once the garlic is cool enough to handle, it can be stored in two ways:

• **Storing whole heads**. The whole heads or individual cloves can be frozen intact. The heads should be wrapped in plastic wrap and placed in a plastic bag. Zipper locking bags work best. For individual cloves place into a plastic bag and pack tightly but keep cloves in one layer. Press out as much air as possible and seal bag tight. You will have packets of garlic purée just waiting to be liberated. They are now ready to be frozen.

• **Storing the purée**. I prefer to remove the garlic from the skins. With a gentle squeeze the garlic will pop out of the skins. For a large batch use a potato ricer to squeeze the garlic. Either technique will result in a smooth **garlic purée**. I find the best way to store the **garlic purée** is to fill a zipper-locking bag. Flatten the bag so it is about $^3/_4$ inches thick; and be sure to burp the bag! (See p.52.) The garlic is now ready to be frozen. It's easy to cut a piece of purée from the bag. Be sure to rewrap tightly before returning to freezer.

Whichever method you use, be sure to save the **garlic skins**. They are full of flavor and can be used to infuse nectars and stocks with rich garlic flavor.

Onions and Shallots

Onions are used ubiquitously in so many cuisines they are sometimes taken for granted. They have a strong supporting role in many dishes, but—slow cooked with fresh herbs until they caramelize—they can step into the spotlight and bring down the house! If you haven't eaten a caramelized onion tart, you are in for a real treat.

There are many kinds of onions—white, standard yellow, plump Spanish, red, and—the Rolls Royces of onions—supersweet Vidalia and Maui. Onions benefit from a long slow cooking which develops their natural sweet flavor. Onions do a disappearing act as they cook, shrinking about 80 percent of their volume. The longer you cook them, the sweeter and darker they will become, as the natural sugars caramelize.

We will make two different onion preparations with different cooking times: basic sautéed onions and caramelized onions. *Basic sautéed onions*, cooked for about ½ hour, can be used in almost all sauces and soups. And for the ultimate onion we will cook them until they turn a dark brown and become ready for their star turn as *caramelized onions*. Once the onions are cooked, the building blocks can be frozen with great success.

Basic Sautéed Onions and Caramelized Onions

Both cooking methods start off the same way:
1. Peel the onions.

2. Slice or chop the onions. I like to slice them because sliced onions are more versatile. You can always chop the sliced onions later, if the recipe calls for chopped.

3. For every 2 cups of tightly packed onions use 1 tablespoon of olive oil, infused olive oil, or olive oil-based marinade (pp.44-47). Cook the sliced onions in the olive oil. I prefer to use a heavy-bottomed, enameled cast iron pan. Start cooking over a medium-high heat. When the onions begin to sizzle, stir, reduce the heat to a lower flame, cover and cook for one half hour. Stir them, scraping the bottom of the pan every 5 minutes or so to prevent sticking and scorching. They are now ready to use in the supporting cast of soups and sauces as *basic sautéed onions*.

Caramelized Onions

To *caramelize* the onions, follow steps 1 to 3 above; however, you must be sure to cook the onions on a low flame. Then continue with step 4:

4. Cook the onions until they are meltingly soft, stirring them every 10 to 15 minutes. Adding $1/2$ teaspoon of sugar per 2 cups of onions will aid the caramelization. This process will take several hours, so it's a good idea to have a good book or other tasks to attend to while they cook. The onions are ready to use when they are meltingly soft and brown.

Caramelized onions are delicious just as they are. They can also be sliced or chopped and used wherever onions are called for in the recipes.

Shallots

Shallots have a similar flavor to onions, but a bit more intense. They can be used interchangeably with onions in any recipe. Shallots may be prepared in the same way as onions. The sauté method for onions can be used with great success for shallots. Peel and slice the shallots, and proceed as in the basic sautéed onion method. Shallots can also be pan-sautéed and caramelized like onions.

Leeks

Leeks add their delicious flavor and texture to many dishes and star in some fantastic soups and tarts. One of the most wonderful sights in Paris or Provence is the piles of long white leeks at the outdoor markets. Europeans prize the leek, and in Europe wonderful specimens abound. Good leeks can be found in the United States, too, but you have to look more carefully. Leeks should be firm, crisp, vibrant; the white part should be at least 6 inches long and, if you are lucky, longer. The white is the most useful part of the leek, although leek greens are wonderful for flavoring stocks. We will use everything but the roots! Puréed leeks add a creamy texture to a recipe, without all the fat of real cream.

The most important thing to remember when preparing leeks is that they must be properly cleaned. This is not difficult—just cut the leek where the white bottom part meets the upper green part. Save the greens for your stock pot, but be sure to wash them as well. Trim the root end but do not cut it off entirely. This will make slicing it easier later, as the pieces will not unravel.

Slow-Cooked Leeks Building Block

1. Starting ¼ inch beyond the root end of the leek, make a cut down the length of the leek; turn the leek 90° and make another cut so we have 4 sections held together by the root end.

2. Under a running faucet, wash the leek, cut-end up, to rinse any dirt or sand from between the cut sections. Leeks can be very gritty, so be meticulous here. Grit in cooked leeks can ruin a dish.

3. Shake excess water from the leeks and lay them flat on a cutting board.

4. Cut the leeks into ⅛-inch slices.

5. For each cup of chopped leeks, add 1 tablespoon olive oil, infused olive oil, or one of the olive oil-based marinades (pp.44-47).

6. Use a heavy-bottomed pot or frying pan and cook the leeks over a low heat, covered, stirring every 5 minutes, scraping the bottom of the pan to prevent them from sticking. Cook for about 45 minutes until they are soft and translucent. Slow cooking develops their flavor and creamy texture. They are now ready to use.

Peppers

Roasted peppers can star in their own culinary drama or be an important part of the supporting cast. Properly handled, they have a rich and delicious flavor and texture and are very easy to prepare. The best and easiest peppers to roast are hefty bell peppers with smooth, shiny, unblemished skins. They come in green, red, yellow, and even orange—sometimes in combinations of these colors. Summer is when you will find them at their peak. They are available year round, although they can be expensive in winter. Prepare a big batch in summer, and freeze them for when the cold winds start to blow.

The traditional way to roast a pepper is to char it over an open flame, turning it slowly to blister the skin all over. This approach is fine if you're a frustrated Boy Scout or you always wanted to be a Campfire Girl.

A much easier, faster, and more efficient way to roast peppers is in a hot oven. The results are fantastic. Just follow these easy steps:

Roasted Peppers Building Block

1. Pre-heat the oven to 400°.

2. Wash any dirt off the peppers—be extra careful to wash around the stem end. Shake the excess water from them and dry with a dish towel or paper towels.

3. Line a cookie sheet with a piece of aluminum foil—heavy duty foil works best. Lightly brush the pan with olive oil or spray it with a non-stick spray. Be sure to roll the foil up the sides of the pan to retain any pepper juices that may be released during the cooking process if the peppers are accidentally broken.

4. Roast the peppers in a pre-heated 400° oven until the skins blister—50 minutes to one hour. Turn the peppers during the cooking—be careful to avoid splitting them—you want to keep the pepper nectar inside the peppers as much as possible. If the peppers do split, do not despair—they will still be delicious. Turning the peppers will insure that they blister evenly. Look for a light brown-colored skin, well blistered, but be careful not to burn them. If the oven is too hot, the skin will burn before the peppers cook properly. If peppers burn, the wonderful nectar inside the peppers will have a bitter taste. Overcooked peppers become too soft and difficult to handle.

5. Remove the peppers from the oven. Fold up the sides of the foil to make a tent with the peppers inside. Seal up the top and sides of the tent and let the peppers cool. They will steam a little, and this will make the skin removal much easier. Allow to sit for 15 minutes.

6. Open the foil carefully. The peppers will have released a wonderful nectar and we want to save every drop! Pour off this liquid and taste it. If the peppers have not been overcooked, it should have a sweet pepper flavor. Set aside.

7. Split the peppers and allow any nectar to drain out. Add to the nectar you've already set aside.

8. Our task now is to remove the skins and seeds. While tomato seeds are unwelcome, pepper seeds are really gross in the finished dish. One can only imagine what the Duchess would have to say about finding one in her food—the mind reels! Think of them as wire coat hangers in your closet. The best way to remove the skin is to pull it off with the aid of a small paring knife. It should pull off very easily. Swish the peppers in the pepper nectar to remove the seeds. You can strain it afterwards to remove the seeds. When done, return the peppers to the nectar.

A faster way to remove the skin and seeds is to run the peppers under cool water. This aids the skin removal and washes away the seeds. Place a strainer or colander under the faucet to collect the seeds and skins as they come off. This will make for an easier cleanup. The one problem with this method is that it also removes some of the flavor. Both methods work well. While the pepper nectar method is more time-consuming, it will result in a more flavorful product. Feel free to use the running water method if you're short of time. Just be sure to drain the peppers well and return them to the nectar. The peppers are now ready to use in our recipes. They can be left as is, chopped into a dice, or puréed into a smooth pepper paste.

Cooked peppers freeze fabulously. If frozen raw they would be a mushy mess. Cooking changes their texture to a silkier, denser one, and freezing has little effect on its quality.

Mushrooms

A pan full of mushrooms sizzling in olive oil with a sprinkling of fresh thyme and rosemary and a grind of black pepper promises great taste to come. Besides their distinctive flavor mushrooms have a wonderful texture. They can be eaten alone or can add to a great variety of dishes.

Some of my fondest childhood memories are of going mushrooming in the woods of Staten Island with my old world grandfather Dominic. Before the Verrazano bridge was built there were lots of woodlands full of mushrooms; he knew which ones were edible and which ones were not. We would bring them to my grandmother who would clean and sauté them with garlic in olive oil. The whole house would fill with their earthy aroma. Happy feasting would soon follow...

If you are lucky enough to live near a source of wild mushrooms, be sure to go hunting with a knowledgeable mycologist. This is not an area with room for mistakes! For most of us our source will be a supermarket, a green grocer, or a farmers' market.

Fresh mushrooms are highly perishable, but once they are cooked they will keep several days. Cooked mushrooms can also be frozen for our frozen pantry. Freezing raw mushrooms would render them a soggy, mushy mess, but cooking them, in any of the forms shown here, transforms them into a very freezable form.

There are many kinds of mushrooms: the standard white, also known as the Paris mushroom, and all the "wild" ones such as cremini, shiitaki, portobello, oyster, chanterel, morel and—if you are lucky enough to find and rich enough to afford—porcini. New varieties are arriving at the market all the time. Mushrooms also come in dried form; we will be using dried porcini (the Italian name) or cèpes (the French name) in some of our recipes. Look for fresh, velvety, unblemished mushrooms with smooth, plump caps. White and cremini mushrooms should have tightly closed caps. The gills of portobello and shiitaki should be intact and bruise-free, and a uniform color. Oyster mushrooms come in clumps and should be full with an even cream color.

Cleaning and Preparing Mushrooms

Different varieties of mushrooms require different techniques for cleaning. All mushrooms benefit from a "dry cleaning," that is, using as little water as possible. How much cleaning you do will depend on how much dirt and grit they harbor.

To clean *white* mushrooms and *cremini* mushrooms, first wipe them with a damp cloth or paper towel. If that is not sufficient, just brush off the excess dirt with a brush. I like using a 2 inch natural bristle paint brush. Sometimes white and cremini mushrooms are so gritty, a quick bath is the only way to render them grit-free. Fill a bowl with cold tap water. Have a colander at the ready. Plunge the mushrooms in, a handful at a time. Rub and swish them, then remove them to the colander to drain. Change the water from time to time as it gets dirty. Blot them on a cookie sheet lined with paper towels.

Sometimes the bottom of the stem has not been trimmed and has dirt still attached to the roots. Just trim this part off, cutting only as much as is necessary.

The entire mushroom can be cooked intact, i.e., the cap and the stem together. For a more elegant result, remove the stems and use just the caps, sliced or whole. Save those stems! They can be chopped and sautéed, or used to flavor stocks.

For *shiitaki* and *portobello* mushrooms, first cut the stem off, flush with the base of the cap. Save the stems. While we won't sauté them with the caps, they will be used to flavor stocks. Starting from the center of the mushroom, brush across the top and then the bottom to remove any bits of grit. I like to cut the shiitaki into $1/8$ inch slices and the portobello into $1/4$ inch slices.

Oyster mushrooms are often very free of any grit, but I turn the clump over and brush down across the bottom and give the top side a quick brush if necessary. The mushroom caps must be separated from the stalks; cut as close as you can and again save any stalks for the stock pot. Depending on the size of the mushrooms, either use them whole or cut them in half lengthwise.

Chanterelles are often gritty, so they need a good brushing with a soft bristled brush—a toothbrush works well. The stems can be tough, so they should be trimmed and saved. The caps can be cooked whole.

Morels usually need only a quick brushing and a quick trim of the ends. But be careful—they can be full of surprises. Once, I cut one open and found it was full of ants, temporarily stunned by being in the refrigerator. They quickly came to life, running all over the cutting board! Morels can be chopped, cut lengthwise, or cooked whole.

Porcini mushrooms usually need only a quick wipe with a damp towel. Cut them into ¼-inch slices. One problem with porcini is that they are sometimes full of worms—yuk! My advice is to break open the cap at the store. It's a real drag to come home to find you paid $35 a pound for wormy mushrooms, and it does nothing to enhance your appetite.

Cooking mushrooms

To cook mushrooms, use a large sauté pan. For best results it's best not to crowd the mushrooms. When they are too crowded, they sweat and produce excess liquid. The goal is to get them brown, which brings out their best flavor. I like to cook each different type of mushroom separately.

Heat the pan and add olive oil—1 tablespoon for each cup of sliced mushrooms. Add the mushrooms when one piece tossed into the oil sizzles. Remember, do not overcrowd. Toss the mushrooms in the oil, turning the mushrooms as they cook. For extra flavor, add some fresh chopped herbs—rosemary and thyme are great, and a pinch of sage or oregano can be used also. About 1 teaspoon of herbs for each cup of mushrooms will add a welcome flavor. Or, use one of the olive oil-based marinades or infused oils from the marinade section, (p.43), omitting the acid.

Cook until the mushrooms are lightly browned.

Duxelle of mushrooms

This mushroom building block calls for shredding, squeezing, and sautéing the mushrooms. Either white or cremini mushrooms may be used. A combination of the two is ideal.

1. Clean the mushrooms

2. Using a food processor with a shredding disk, process the mushrooms. Alternatively, you can finely pulse-chop the mushrooms with the cutting blade.

3. Place 1 cup of grated or chopped mushrooms at a time in the center of a clean dish towel or a length of cheesecloth that has been triple-folded. Wrap and squeeze out as much liquid as possible. Save the liquid to add to a sauce or stock.

   Continue in batches until all the mushrooms have been squeezed.

4. You may want to add 1-2 tablespoons of chopped raw shallots per cup of mushrooms.

5. In a sauté pan, sauté 1 tablespoon olive oil, marinade, or infused oil per cup of mushrooms. Cook, stirring frequently, until the mushrooms are lightly browned.

6. The extracted juice may be added to a stock or soup, or reduced by 80% and mixed back into the mushroom mixture after the initial sautéing. Cook for a few minutes more.

If the squeezing step seems too onerous, you can skip it and just sauté the mushrooms until all the liquid is evaporated. While this recipe is traditionally made with white or cremini mushrooms, you can also use portobello, shiitake, or chanterelles.

Porcini mushroom essence

Dried porcini mushrooms, crèpes in French, are easy to work with. Just follow these steps to make the essence.

1. Cover the mushrooms in water heated just below the boil, and soak about $1/2$ hour. Press the mushrooms down into the soaking liquid with a fork from time to time as they cool.

2. The mushrooms always have bits of dirt or sand on them, so we must be sure to soak it off the mushrooms before using them. When the soaking liquid has cooled, remove the mushrooms from the liquid, swishing them as you remove them. *Save the soaking liquid.*

3. I like to give the mushrooms a second bath in cold water, again swishing them to remove any last bits of sand. *Save the second soaking liquid and add it to the first.*

4. The mushrooms are now ready to use in sauces and soups, or you can combine them with the strained soaking liquid to create an intensely flavored mushroom essence.

5. To make the mushroom essence, strain the soaking liquid through several layers of cheese cloth. The soaking liquid is culinary gold. Pour carefully—the dirt will have settled to the bottom. You may want to avoid the last dregs, which will have the most sand.

6. Boil the mushroom essence to reduce its volume by $2/3$. In a blender purée the mushroom essence and reconstituted mushrooms. Remember that when putting hot food into a blender, you must start the machine with the lid ajar and process with a low speed, or the steam will send the mixture splattering over the kitchen.

The essence is now ready to use.

Other Vegetables

Several vegetables can make good building blocks that will facilitate quick and delicious recipes. These include potatoes, members of the pumpkin and squash family, eggplant, dried beans, and green vegetables like spinach, broccoli, and peas. Most of these will be puréed, with the exception of the beans, which will be left whole for storage.

Potatoes

The best kinds of potatoes to use for building blocks are Idaho or Yukon Gold. These are cheap and plentiful. Save the heirloom and exotic varieties for sautéing and roasting with our marinades and infused oils. Choose potatoes that are firm and free of green patches or sprouts, with skin that is smooth and unblemished. Cooked potatoes will keep very well in the refrigerator for a few days or in the freezer for a few months.

The best way to prepare the potatoes as a building block is to boil and purée them. Traditionally, potatoes are put into cold water, which is then brought to the boil. I prefer to infuse the water with herbs and aromatic vegetables first. This approach lets the potatoes absorb the herbs' and vegetables' flavors while they cook. Just follow this easy method...

Potato Purée

5 pounds Idaho or Yukon Gold potatoes, or a mixture, well peeled. No dark spots, missed skin bits, or wayward eyes need apply!
bay leaves
6-8 branches fresh thyme
a handful of garlic cloves.
1 onion, cut in half
1 carrot, peeled
1-2 stalks celery, rough-chopped in 1-inch pieces
cold tap water
1 teaspoon sea salt

1. Place the herbs and vegetables in a pot large enough to hold all the potatoes.

2. Fill the pot half-full of water.

3. Bring to a boil. Reduce the heat and simmer for half an hour.

4. Add the potatoes and enough additional water so the potatoes are barely covered.

5. Bring back to a boil. Reduce to a simmer.

6. Cook until the potatoes are just tender but not falling apart.

7. Drain the potatoes. Discard the vegetables and herbs. Press the potatoes and garlic through a potato ricer or food mill. Some of the thyme leaves will also pass through with the potato purée. This not a problem, as they add a delightful flavor and aren't nasty to the bite.

8. Repeat the ricing process to insure a lump-free purée, or don't repeat, depending on your time and inclination.

Some chefs pass the purée through a *tamis*, a fine wire mesh-covered drum. But unless you have a galley slave on hand or the queen herself is coming to dinner, stick to the old-fashioned ricer!

The potato purée is now ready to be used for fabulous potato soups (pp.82-83). For terrific mashed potatoes, stir in ½ cup of infused olive oil (p.45), 2 tablespoons garlic puree (p.19), and 1½ cups infused milk (p.116).

Pumpkins and Winter Squash

Pumpkins and squash, including butternut, acorn, hubbard, dumpling, and kabocha (my favorite) lend themselves to the building-block method. I like to steam, microwave, or roast them, purée the flesh, and then use them as a side vegetable, or to create a wonderful soup. They lend themselves to the creation of custards, which can be savory or sweet. Pumpkins and squash also make a delicious warm bed for fish or fowl.

Microwaved or Steamed Squash or Pumpkin

The easiest way to cook squash or pumpkins is to cut them in half, scrape out the seeds, place cut side down on a plate and micro-zap until the flesh is tender, about 10-20 minutes, depending on the size of the squash and the strength of your microwave. Squash can also be cooked whole, but be sure to puncture to avoid an explosion. The squash can also be steamed. Allow to cool enough to handle, then scrape out the flesh with a spoon. Pumpkins and some squash can be very watery when cooked. If the cooked flesh is watery, let it drain in a colander, saving the liquid to add to a soup base. Purée the flesh in a food processor. It's now ready to use.

Roasted Squash or Pumpkin Purée

Roasting intensifies the flavor of squash or pumpkin and makes a drier purée.

1. Prepare as for microwaved squash above.

2. Brush with an herb marinade or infused oil. (pp.44-45)

3. Line a baking sheet with foil. Place squash cut-side-up on the foil.

4. Roast in a 350° oven until tender—35 to 40 minutes.

5. Purée the flesh in a food processor.

Green Vegetables

Almost any green vegetable can be blanched and puréed to form a building block, ready to be used as a vegetable side dish or as the base for soups, custards, and quiches. Some of the vegetables that work best here are broccoli, peas, string beans, spinach, and brussel sprouts. All green vegetables can be prepared by the blanch and refresh method:

Blanch and Refresh Preparation

1. Clean and wash the vegetable.

2. Drop in boiling, lightly salted water. Cook until the desired tenderness is reached. Remember, slightly *al dente* is the best now, since you will be reheating later.

3. As soon as the desired tenderness is reached, drain and immediately run *cold* water over them. This accomplishes two things. First, it stops the cooking. Second it will set the color a bright, natural green. If you don't do this, the vegetables will turn a dull, yucky olive green, looking oh so tired—I'm yawning!

4. Drain the vegetables in a colander, then on paper towels to absorb excess moisture. Spinach needs to be squeezed against the side of the colander in order to drain fully.

The wonderful thing about this method is that when you reheat the vegetables, they will keep that vibrant green color.

To make building blocks, we purée the vegetables. There are several reasons for this. First, puréed vegetables are a delight to eat. They are more appreciated in Europe, but just as we Americans love the creamy texture of mashed potatoes, puréed vegetables can have the same sensuous feel in the mouth. They make a wonderful addition to the "comfort food" family. Second, the puréed vegetables blend well into the soups, sauces, custards, and quiches, in which we will be using them. Third, puréed vegetables are easier to pack tightly to avoid air pockets which result in the bane of the frozen pantry, the dreaded *freezer burn*. A food processor is indispensable for the task of puréeing vegetables.

To purée, fill the processor bowl half full with the well-drained vegetables. I like to add 1 tablespoon olive oil per cup of vegetable. This makes for a smoother, richer result. Process until smooth. A bit of roasted garlic is always welcome.

Just a grind of fresh pepper and a shake of salt, and the purée is ready to eat as a vegetable side dish, or to be used as a building block.

Eggplant

Eggplant can make a great side dish, a dip, a wonderful soup, or a warm bed for a sautéed chicken breast or a slice of veal. It combines well with some of the other building blocks. It's very easy to make a batch of eggplant purée by roasting the eggplant. As with peppers, some people like to roast them over an open flame, charring the skin on the plant—and your fingers, too, if you're not careful! It's much easier to roast them in the oven.

Roasted Eggplant Purée

1. Wash the eggplants, being careful of the stem, which can have small thorns that hurt! Pat them dry. Prick them in a few places so they don't explode.

2. Line a cookie sheet or flat pan with foil. Lay the eggplants down and roast them in a 350° oven until they are tender when pierced with a fork, about ½ to one hour, depending on their size.

3. Allow to cool. Slice open, scoop out the flesh, and put in a colander or strainer to drain for 15-20 minutes.

4. Purée the flesh in a food processor until smooth. Voilà, it's now ready to be used.

Beans

When beans and lentils are cooked in an herb and aromatic vegetable-infused bath, the results are delicious legume building blocks that will find their way into soups, salads, dips, and purées.

There are many different kinds of beans, and all can be cooked by the herb and aromatic vegetable-infused bath method. The beans that are of particular interest to us are the Italian cannelli or their American cousins the Great Northern, also black or turtle beans, garbanzo beans or chickpeas, French flageolets, and tiny green French lentils.

There are many ways to cook the beans, but the best way is to simmer them gently in a rich herb and vegetable stock. You can use the vegetable stock from the stock recipe section (p.39) or put together a special bath of herbs and vegetables to cook with the beans.

If you are making a stock specifically for the beans, it is best to simmer the herbs and vegetables together first, before adding the beans, to extract as much flavor out of them as possible. This will result in very flavorful beans

Herb and Aromatic Vegetable Bath for Beans

To make a rich stock in which to cook the beans, assemble the following:

(All the vegetables should be well washed and rough chopped:)

1 cup celery

1 cup carrots, well scrubbed or peeled

1 cup onions with stem ends removed. It is not necessary to peel the onions.

1 head of garlic, separated. Crush the indivual cloves, but it is not necessary to peel them. Or, use 2 cups roasted garlic skins, left over from roasting garlic (p.19)

3-4 branches of thyme

1-2 branches of rosemary

4-5 fresh sage leaves

1-2 bay leaves

$1/4$ teaspoon whole peppercorns

$1/4$ cup olive oil

In addition, you may add any or all of the following to make an even better stock.

Leek greens

Red or green pepper scraps

Italian parsley stalks, crushed

1. Place all the ingredients together in a thick-bottomed pot. Sauté the vegetables for 15 minutes in the olive oil. Add 4 quarts of cold water.

2. Bring to a boil, reduce to a strong simmer and cook for one hour.

3. Strain the stock.

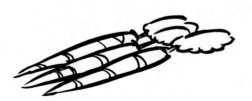

Beans: Herb and Aromatic Vegetable-Infused Bath Preparation

1. All beans must be carefully picked over to remove any stones or "off" beans that may be in the batch. One missed stone could ruin your day, to say nothing of your teeth! Rinse them in cold water and drain.

2. Beans should be soaked before cooking or they will have a tendency to burst their skins when you cook them. Cover them by two inches of cold water and let them soak overnight. If you are in a hurry, cover them with boiling water and let them soak for one hour. After soaking the beans, drain them, and rinse them with cold water.

3. Cover the beans with stock to a height of one inch above the beans. Bring the stock to a boil. Immediately reduce the stock to a simmer. If you cook the beans on too high a flame, they will burst. Our goal is for the beans to absorb the delicious stock, become nice and plump, but not burst their skins. Cook until the beans are very tender. This will take approximately 30-40 minutes depending on the size and age of the beans.

4. Strain the beans and save the liquid. This will stop the beans from cooking. The beans can be stored in the liquid once it has cooled. If you are going to refrigerate or freeze them, cover them with the cooking liquid.

Of course, once you have cooked up a batch of beans, it would be a shame not to make a little bean salad or bean salad purée while the beans are still warm.(pp.65-66).

Lentils

There is really no comparison between the flavor and texture of French green lentils, with their wonderful nutty taste, and the standard dark brown lentils we know from Joe's Diner. French green lentils are worth the extra expense.

Lentils, like beans, should be picked over to remove any stones. Lentils do not need to be soaked, but will benefit from an herb and vegetable infused simmer. Lentils cook quickly and will not take more than 20 minutes. Bring them to a boil in the stock and then reduce to a simmer. They should remain a little *al dente*. Strain the liquid and allow it to cool. The lentils are ready to be used.

Stocks

A pot full of aromatic vegetables, fresh herbs, and chicken or beef simmering on the stove will make your kitchen smell divine. Once you have made a good stock, soups and sauces are just a quick simmer away. Stocks may be reduced to concentrate the flavor and take up less storage space in the freezer.

Vegetable Stock

You can accumulate these ingredients in the freezer in a bag reserved for making vegetable stock. Base your stock on what you have available. The more of these ingredients you have on hand, the better the stock will be.

2 cups scraped or peeled carrots, rough chopped
2 cups onions, root end removed, rough chopped. It is not
    necessary to peel them.
2 cups leek greens, well washed, rough chopped
1 cup celery stalks and leaves, well washed, rough chopped
1 cup seeded, chopped green pepper
1 cup flat-leaf parsley stalks
1 head of garlic, well crushed. It is not necessary to peel, but
    ditch the root end.
(or a handful of roasted garlic skins if you have made garlic
    puree see page 19))
1 medium-sized parsnip, peeled and chopped
1 head of Romaine or Boston lettuce, washed
1/2 cup basil leaves
1-2 cups mushroom stems
5-6 branches fresh thyme
1/2 teaspoon black peppercorns
2 bay leaves
1 teaspoon sea salt
3 tablespoons extra virgin olive oil
1 cup rough-chopped ripe and fresh plum or Roma tomatoes,
    or 1 cup tomato skins leftover from making concasse toma-
    toes. (p.11)
4 quarts cold tap water
1-2 cups dry white wine or vermouth (optional)

1. In an 8 quart stock pot heat the olive oil over medium heat.

2. Add all the ingredients except the tomatoes, water, and wine.

3. Cook, stirring occasionally, until the vegetables are softened, about 15 minutes.

4. Add the tomatoes, water, and wine. Bring to a boil, then reduce to a simmer.

5. Simmer for 45 minutes to one hour.

6. Strain stock into a clean pot or bowl. Allow the remains to drain well. Press down with a spoon to extract as much stock as possible. Now strain through cheesecloth or a clean dish towel to remove any sand. *Voilà*—a delicious vegetable stock that even the most carnivorous eaters will enjoy!

"Like mama used to make ... or should have!"

Chicken Stock

6 pounds raw chicken bones and meat, such as chicken backs, necks, gizzards, and, if possible chicken feet. Leftover roast chicken bones can be added. Also, if you have a duck or turkey neck saved, throw it in.

1 pound veal bones (optional, but will add flavor and gelatine for a richer stock)

3 cups rough chopped onions, root end removed. It's not necessary to peel them.

3 cups peeled, rough-chopped carrots

2 cups rough chopped, scrubbed celery stalks and leaves

1 cup leek greens, well washed

1 medium parsnip, peeled and rough chopped

1 head of garlic, crushed. Remove stem end. Or 3-4 heads of garlic skins, if you have made garlic purée, (see p.19)

1 cup flat-leaf parsley stalks

1-2 cup mushroom stems (if available)

2 bay leaves

4-5 branches fresh thyme leaves

½ teaspoon black peppercorns

6 quarts water

1. Place bones and chicken parts in a 10 quart stock pot. Pour over them 6 quarts of cold tap water. Turn heat on high to bring to a boil. Then immediately reduce to a simmer—if you boil the stock too rapidly, it will become cloudy.

2. The bones and meat will release scum and fat. Periodically skim them from the surface, or the stock will become cloudy.

3. After 1 hour of simmering and skimming, add all the vegetables, herbs, salt, and pepper. Continue to simmer for 2-4 hours.

4. Strain the stock into a bowl or pot using a colander.

5. Clean the original pot and restrain the stock back into it through a piece of cheesecloth that has been wet and wrung out or a Chinoise strainer to remove any little bits. This will produce a beautiful, clear stock.

6. Return the stock to a simmer and reduce by half. This will make storage easier and result in a very rich stock. The concentrated stock will work very well for sauces. For soup—just reconstitute with an equal amount of water.

This recipe should be used as a guide. You may adjust the ingredients to suit your taste. If you are garlic-mad like me, you may want to increase the amount of garlic in the stock.

Beef Stock

5 pounds shin bones and shin meat or chuck. Use the most
   inexpensive cut you can find. Meat and bones should be cut
   into 3-4 inch pieces
1 pound veal bones, cut into 3-4-inch pieces
3 cups peeled carrots, cut into 2-inch pieces
4-5 medium yellow onions, peeled and cut in half
8 ribs of celery, scrubbed and cut into 2-inch pieces.
1 parsnip, peeled and cut into 2-inch pieces
6 quarts cold tap water
2 bay leaves
1 level teaspoon black peppercorns
4-5 sprigs thyme
1-2 heads garlic, crushed
(a handful of roasted garlic skins, if you have made garlic puree,
   p.19)
1½ cups fresh, ripe tomato, cut into 2-inch chunks
optional: 1 handful leek greens
optional: 1 handful flat leaf parsley stalks
optional: 1 bottle dry white wine

Note: if you are a real carnivore, and enjoy rib-roasts and the like, save those bones and cooking juices to add to the stock pot.

1. Pre-heat oven to 400°.
2. Use a non-stick spray on a roasting pan large enough to hold the bones, meat, and vegetables in a single layer. Use 2 pans if necessary.
3. Place the bones and meat in the pan and oven roast for 20-30 minutes.
4. After 20-30 minutes add carrots, onions, celery, and parsnips. Mix to coat with fat. Roast another 15-20 minutes, until everything is nicely browned. Be very careful not to burn the bones, meat, or vegetables.
5. Pour off the fat and place bones, meat, and vegetables in a stock pot.
6. Add a cup of water to the roasting pan. Scrape and swish to dislodge any tasty bits. Add them to the stock pot.
7. Pour the cold water over the ingredients in the pot.
8. Bring to a boil, then reduce to a simmer.
9. Skim off scum and foam as it rises to the surface.
10. Let the stock simmer for 2 hours.
11. After 2 hours, add bay leaf, thyme, peppercorns, garlic, tomato, and any of the optional ingredients.
12. Simmer 2 more hours.
13. Strain the stock; a Chinoise will remove all but the liquid

14. At this point I like to reduce the stock further. This will concentrate the flavor and make the sauce easier to store.

15. You may wish to cook down the stock to a demi-glace, a thick syrup of very intense beef flavor. You may reconstitute it with water to make a beef broth or use it as is for an intense sauce.

Canned Chicken, Beef, or Vegetable Stock

In the event you find yourself in need of stock and don't have time to make it yourself, you may use canned stock, if you enhance it as follows (and promise to make a big batch of real stock as soon as fate will allow).

Add to the canned stock a selection of all the vegetables and herbs listed above and simmer together for a least $1/2$ hour. Strain and use. It will not be as good as the home-made stock, but in a pinch it will be passable. Just don't expect any standing ovations for your finished dish.

Marinades, Infused Oils, and infused Vinegars

Marinades are liquid flavor zaps that elevate flavors from good to great. A marinade can turn an ordinary chicken breast from a good source of protein into a real taste treat. The marinades we will discuss are based on combinations of fresh herbs, garlic, pepper, and sometimes citrus juice, vinegar, or wine. Fowl, meat, fish, and vegetables each have a marinade bath that will make their turn before the fire even more delightful to the taste buds.

If you frequent fancy food shops or peruse "gourmet" catalogues, you will see flavored oils and vinegars offered at steep prices. It is very easy to make your own infused oils and vinegars to use in cooking or to drizzle over vegetables, salads, and soups. Always use the best quality oils and Vinegars. Life is too short to use poor quality oils and vinegars! All of these make great gifts for family and friends.

Marinades

What I love about making marinades is that you can make a cup or two and, since you only need a few tablespoons at time, you can store the rest in small packages in the freezer. The frozen marinade will defrost in seconds in your microwave or in a hot water bath. I like to keep a variety of them on hand to suit my whim of the moment.

The marinade I use most often is based on those tried and true herbs of Provence and Italy—rosemary, thyme, bay leaf, and garlic. There are no exact proportions. You can increase or decrease the amounts according to your taste.

Basic Marinade

1 cup extra virgin olive oil

heaping $\frac{1}{4}$ cup thyme leaves

$\frac{1}{4}$ cup rosemary leaves

4-10 cloves garlic (not necessary to peel)

2 bay leaves

1 teaspoon fresh ground pepper

Now, a hot tip: save all the residue left in the strainer. Bang it into a pot, rinse the blender jar, and add to the pot. Bring to a boil and simmer $\frac{1}{2}$ hour. Strain and save the liquid—it's great for cooking pasta, polenta, or potatoes, or poaching shrimp or lobsters. If you don't need it right away, reduce it to a cup or two, cool it, and freeze for another time. Nothing wasted!

If you have a scullery maid to pick off all the leaves of the thyme and rosemary, God bless you; for the rest of us, I have a quick and easy solution. It requires the use of a blender—a food processor doesn't do as thorough a job.

1. Break off the herb leaves roughly, trying to avoid the fatter twigs, and put them in the blender. Especially with the rosemary, you needn't worry about getting rid of the smaller twigs.

2. Add the olive oil, pepper, and garlic cloves, cover the blender jar, and zap on the highest speed for 5 minutes until all the contents have been pulverized.

3. Pour the liquid mixture through a strainer and press with a wooden spoon to extract as much of the oil and herb mixture as possible.

Voilà, your marinade is ready to use!

Variations:

Variations on the basic marinade include:

- Changing the ratio of thyme to rosemary, or using just one or the other.

- Certain other herbs may be added depending on the intended use. If you are lucky enough or smart enough to buy or grow lemon thyme, it makes a super marinade for chicken or fish. Use lemon thyme, garlic, and olive oil.

- When the marinade is to be used for chicken, lamb, or pork, fresh sage leaves are a welcome addition to the mix. Sage is a strong herb, so go easy. I find one part sage to three parts thyme makes an ideal blend.

- Sometimes I like a very simple mixture of rosemary, olive oil, and pepper, especially for a delicate fish like salmon or trout, where garlic would overwhelm the delicate flavor.

- For meat and fowl I sometimes like to add a tablespoon of one or two of the following: lemon juice, orange juice, white wine, sherry, lime juice, or vinegar (balsamic, red, or white). Do not use these additions if you intend this marinade for fish, as the acid will start to break down the flesh and make the fish mushy. The tenderizing effect of these ingredients is more welcome on meat and fowl.

Herb-Infused Oils

I like to have a variety of infused oils on hand. There are countless possible combinations of herbs to add to an oil infusion. For our recipes, we will make four infusions: basil oil, thyme oil, rosemary oil, and thyme, rosemary, garlic, and bay leaf oil.

In all these recipes the quantities of herbs to use are given as a rough guide. Feel free to increase any of the amounts for a more intense flavor. The herbs, stained from the oil after the infusing, may be used in marinades, stocks, or to infuse water.

Straining the basil oil will result in a delightful bonus—**basil purée**. This is the residue left after the oil is strained from the basil/oil mixture. Basil purée will be very useful for making pesto or for adding flavor to sauces.

Basil oil (and Basil Purée)

Puréeing sweet basil and fine olive oil results in liquid green "gold." Drizzled across the surface of a white bean soup or a perfectly grilled salmon filet, it's the finishing touch that takes the completed dish to the next level. It's very simple to make and results in two different products: basil oil and basil purée. Basil oil should be used "raw"—drizzled on at the last moment before serving. Its color will be that of liquid emeralds.

fresh basil
best quality extra-virgin olive oil

1. Wash and carefully stem the basil. Taste a bit of the leaves before you buy, or pick your own basil, as it can sometimes be a bit harsh or bitter, in which case don't use it.

2. After the basil has been washed, blanch in boiling water for 30 seconds, refresh in cold water, drain, and squeeze out excess water.

3. In a blender add 1 cup of oil for every ½ cup of tightly packed, blanched basil leaves. Purée on high speed until well pulverized.

4. Now, pour into a fine strainer and let the basil oil drain out. Press the purée with a wooden spoon to extract as much oil as possible. The basil oil is ready to use.

5. The **purée** left behind in the strainer is perfect for making pesto sauce, or to flavor a tomato sauce.

Thyme Oil

12 4-inch branches of thyme. Use regular thyme or lemon thyme, or, even better, a mixture.
1 cup extra virgin olive oil

1. Blanch the thyme 30 seconds in boiling water. Refresh in cold water. Dry on a towel.

2. Gently heat the oil until it is warm to the touch but not hot—100° is about right.

3. Place the thyme in the jar of a blender and pour the oil over it. Pulse the blender 3 times for 3 seconds each. The purpose of the pulsing is to bruise the herbs so they will release more of their flavor. Pour into a clean, glass jar with a tight-fitting lid.

4. Allow the oil to cool to room temperature. Cover the jar and let the oil steep in a cool, dark place (not the refrigerator) for 1 week.

5. After this period the oil is ready to use. Strain, and keep the oil refrigerated until you need it.

Rosemary Oil

4-5 5-inch stems rosemary
1 cup extra virgin olive oil

The steps of this recipe are identical to those of the Thyme Oil recipe above...

Thyme, Rosemary, Garlic, and Bay Leaf Oil

2-3 4-inch branches thyme
2-3 5-inch branches rosemary leaves
5-6 firm garlic cloves. Remove loose skin but do not peel.
2-4 bay leaves
1 cup extra virgin olive oil

1. Process thyme and rosemary as in the preceding recipes. Pour into a clean glass jar with a tight-fitting lid.

2. Crack the garlic cloves: lay them on a cutting board and gently smack them with the side of a chef's knife or cleaver. Try to split but not crush them.

3. Add the garlic and bay leaf to the infusing jar.

4. Warm the oil as in the previous recipes.

5. Let the oil and herbs steep for a week in a cool, dark, place (other than the refrigerator).

6. After this period the oil is ready to use. Strain, and keep the oil refrigerated until you need it.

Herb Infused Vinegars

Red and white wine vinegar and sherry wine vinegar are best for infusing with herbs. Balsamic vinegar is better when used "straight." Basil, parsley, tarragon, chervil, thyme, rosemary, oregano, marjoram, bay leaf, garlic, hot peppers, and lemon and orange rind will perfume vinegar with their unique flavors. I recommend buying a case of pint size mason jars and making a selection of herb-vinegar blends. They will keep up to 1 year in a cool, dry place. Some of my favorite blends follow. These recipes are each designed to make just one cup of infused vinegar—that way you can decide for yourself which variation you like best. Then you can easily double or triple the recipe. The herbs are cut into 2-inch pieces so they will fit comfortably in the vinegar bath. If you are using a larger quantity of vinegar, you can have longer pieces of herbs.

All infused vinegars are made the same way:

1. Wash the herbs.
2. Soft herbs like basil, parsley, tarragon, or chervil should be blanched for 30 seconds and refreshed in cold water.
3. Dry the herbs.
4. Place the herbs to be infused in the bottom of a clean glass jar with a tight fitting lid.
5. Pour the vinegar over the herbs to cover. Cover the jar with the lid and tighten. Keep in a cool, dark place to steep for 1 or 2 weeks.
6. The vinegar is ready to use. You may strain the vinegar or not.

Basil Vinegar
1 cup red or white wine vinegar
1/2 cup loose-packed basil leaves, washed and dried
3-4 cracked garlic cloves (optional)
3-4 2-inch strips of orange or lemon rind (optional). Remove with a sharp potato peeler, taking only the outermost part of the skin, avoiding the bitter, white pith. If you cut too deep, scrape off any pith with a small paring knife.

Chervil or Tarragon Vinegar

1 cup white wine vinegar

4-5 branches chervil or tarragon, washed and dried, cut into
    2-inch pieces

Bouquet Garni Vinegar

Thyme, bay leaf, and parsley make up the traditional bouquet garni.
It's a natural combination for an infused vinegar.

1 cup red, white, or sherry wine vinegar

2-3 4-inch branches thyme, cut into 2-inch pieces
2-3 bay leaves
small bunch parsley leaves and stems, cut into 2-inch piece
1/4 teaspoon black peppercorns (optional)
2 2-inch strips lemon rind (optional)
1-2 hot peppers (optional)

Herbs de Provence Vinegar

A mixture of the favorite herbs used in Provence makes a
vibrant vinegar.

2-3 4-inch branches thyme, cut into 2-inch pieces
2 4-inch branches rosemary, cut into 2-inch pieces
1-2 4-inch branches oregano or marjoram
3-4 cloves garlic, cracked
2 bay leaves
3-4 sage leaves
1 cup red or white wine vinegar
2 2-inch strips lemon or orange rind (optional)
2 hot peppers (optional)
1/4 teaspoon black peppercorns (optional)

Sherry Wine Vinegar with Garlic, Thyme, and Bay Leaf

1 cup sherry wine vinegar
2-3 cloves garlic, cracked
3-4 4-inch branches thyme, cut into 2-inch pieces
2 bay leaves
2 2-inch strips lemon or orange rind (optional)

Try your own variations—use your imagination. These vinegars may
be used in any recipe calling for vinegar.

The importance of fresh herbs

I encourage you to consider growing your own herb garden. Whether you use just clay pots on the window sill or make a full-fledged garden section, since most herbs are perennials, they will reward you with years of bounty for a minute amount of care.

Nothing rewards a cook the way fresh herbs do. I remember when I first arrived in Paris to continue my training in cooking. Finding the markets full of all kinds of fresh herbs, I thought *anyone* can make great food as long as they use fresh herbs. Well, for some a little technique will help, but I can't stress enough the fab flavor and goodness fresh herbs will bring. [They are also readily available at your green grocery so go for it.]

You should consider growing the following: rosemary, thyme, lemon thyme, sage, flat leaf parsley, chives, and basil. A small bay leaf tree is also a beautiful idea, if your climate can support it, or, with good light, it can be grown as a houseplant.

There is a genuine satisfaction that comes from picking your own herbs. You will save on the cost of store-bought, and they will be impeccably fresh. But please keep in mind, whatever the source, there is no substitute for fresh herbs.

Packaging the building blocks

Now that you have created all these wonderful building blocks, let me tell you the best ways to package them. The most important thing to remember is that air is the bane of good food preservation. If the frozen food is exposed to air, the result will be the dreaded freezer burn. This meanie will destroy texture and flavor—don't let it happen to you!

The best way to avoid this fate is to package your building blocks in as air-tight a manner as possible. There are several options. But whichever one you choose, the no-air policy is very important.

Vacuum Sealer

The most efficient way to accomplish air-tight packaging. Foodsaver brand makes a good model for around three hundred dollars. It is a bit of an investment, but probably worth it if you plan to use it often. With a vacuum sealer the food is placed in a special plastic bag; then all the air is sucked out, leaving an airtight package. If you can afford the expense of the machine, go for it!

Plastic Containers

Another option. The best I have found are Tupperware and Rubbermaid brands. They stand up to repeated runs through the dishwasher—an important consideration. They come in numerous sizes. The smaller ones are most useful for freezing serving-sized amounts of building blocks. For the stocks some of the larger ones are more useful. The trick to using these containers is to fill them so that when the lid is placed on top there is no room for any air under the lid. This is sometimes a bit difficult to determine, but with a bit of trial and error you will soon master the technique. You must also allow for expansion as the building block freezes.

Zipper Locking Plastic Bag

My favorite container. They come in several sizes, from half-pint to gallon, and are easy to fill and label. They fit into the freezer easily and they do a good job. The trick with using these bags is filling and sealing them. Some of the newer bags are designed to stand up while they are being filled. If not, follow these steps.

1. Open the bag. Turn the top 2 inches of the bag inside out.

2. Slide the bag into a measuring cup or bowl. Pour the building block into the bag.

3. Fold the bag back to the original position and remove from the cup. Seal the bag across, leaving a small ¼-inch space open in one corner. Carefully lay the bag flat and press to extract as much air as possible. When all the air has been removed, close it tight. I call this "burping the bag."

4. For extra protection slide this bag into another one. Reuse these bags, so as not to be wasteful.

Hints:

Use a wide funnel. If you find it difficult to pour the building block into the bag, a wide funnel will be a big help. I use two. One funnel I leave as is—the long down spout attached. I use this for liquids. The other funnel I have modified by cutting the spout off at the base. With plastic funnels, it is very easy to saw off the spout with a hacksaw blade. This creates a funnel with a large hole at the bottom. The wide spout allows more bulky building blocks to fall into the open bag easily.

Planning the use of building blocks. Ideally, you should make packages in the amounts you are most likely to use. For instance, you might freeze stocks in one-quart packages, while storing roasted onions or peppers in ½ cup packages. The ½ pint size plastic bags are ideal for the smaller amounts.

Use a bigger bag and then fold it before freezing. For example, place two cups of sauteed onions in a quart bag; seal tight. Lay the bag flat on a surface. Press the bag in two places to make 3 separate compartments within the same bag. Fold the bag into thirds and freeze. Now when you need to use some, just cut off one section and carefully rewrap the rest. Once cut, I like to wrap the bag in plastic wrap and put it all into a new plastic bag.

Recipes

Sauces

Served over or under your recipe, a sauce can add flavor and texture to a wide variety of foods. Smooth or chunky, thin or thick, from low-fat tomato garlic to high-fat pesto, there is a sauce for you! The various building blocks make preparing sauces quick and easy.

Tomato Sauce

Tomato sauces made with our fresh tomato purée building block are in a completely different league from tomato sauces that come out of a can or a jar. With the basic tomato purée building block we can make a great variety of sauces—the possibilities are endless. The following variations should be considered guidelines. You can have great fun experimenting with the different flavors like a mad culinaire. One thing is certain—once you have developed a taste for sauce made with fresh tomatoes it will be hard to eat anything else!

Basic tomato sauce

Combine ingredients and simmer the sauce until it has been reduced to the desired thickness—by 25% to 50%. For best results make the sauce the day before you want to serve it. This will give the flavors a chance to blend and harmonize.

Variations:

Some other ingredients that will greatly enhance the sauce can be added. As with all the basic ingredients, the amounts given are rough guidelines. Use more or less according to your taste. Fresh and some dried herbs add more complexity to the sauce. Some possibilities are:

Fresh and Dried Herbs

• **Fresh basil** is really a must. ½ cup of fresh chopped basil or 1-2 tablespoons of the basil purée building block (p.46) will add its sweet herbal perfume to make the sauce fragrant. It is hard to imagine tomato sauce without some basil. Add the basil just before the sauce is ready to be used—cooking basil dulls its sweet taste and perfume.

• **Flat leaf Italian parsley** adds fresh herbal flavor to the sauce. (Curly leafed parsley is useless for anything but a tacky garnish.) You can chop the tender parts of the stalks, sauté in a little olive oil and add to the basic sauce. Save the stalks for use in making stock or flavoring tomato juice. Do not just throw them away

Ingredients

1 quart of tomato purée building block—either the beefsteak (p.16) or plum tomato (p.14)

¼ cup roasted garlic purée building block (p.19)

1 cup cooked chopped onions building block (p.21)

salt and pepper to taste

- Use 1 tablespoon fresh **oregano** or 1 teaspoon good quality dried. Oregano is one herb which can be better when used dried. Make sure to use a good quality, freshly packed herb. Old oregano is only good to season a compost heap!

- A pinch of dried **thyme** or **sage** will add an interesting flavor but fresh will be much more robust.

- Use only **fresh rosemary**. Unlike dried oregano, thyme, and sage, dried rosemary lacks the fresh herb's vibrancy and has a nasty texture. I would not use it.

Whichever herbs you use, and I would use them all together, they should be added to the purée before you simmer it—except for the basil. I like to stir in basil at the end for a more intense flavor.

To make more complex tomato sauces consider consider adding some of these ingredients:

- Any of the **mushrooms** discussed in the mushroom chapter except morels would be a fine addition to the sauce. Morrels are expensive and their intense flavor is muted in the tomato sauce. A rough guideline is 1 cup cooked mushrooms or duxelle building block (pp.29-30) per quart of sauce, more or less as taste and pocketbook dictate. Add them to the basic sauce before the half hour simmer. For a more intense mushroom flavor, add ½ cup of the porcini mushroom building block. (p.30)

- The **roasted peppers** building block (p.25) will add a wonderful flavor to the sauce. Add ½ to 1 cup of diced peppers to the sauce. You may want to add some dried **red pepper flakes** if you want to make a spicy sauce—start with a teaspoon. Add before the simmer step.

- **Leeks** are not usually found in tomato sauce but they add a distinctive touch. Use ½ to 1 cup leeks per quart. Add before the simmer step.

- Although we have used both **garlic** and **onions** in the basic recipe, you may increase both of these. I like a very garlic-rich sauce—one half cup of purée per quart.

- **Wine**, either red or white, can be a wonderful flavor enhancer. I like using dry white vermouth, but either a dry red or white will work. One half to one cup works well. Add before the simmer step.

- **Meat** sauces, known as Bolognese or Ragu, are very popular. You can use beef, veal, or pork, ground or cut into small cubes. It can be interesting to use a combination of these meats. A pound of meat per quart of sauce will work well.

Preparing Meat Sauces:

1. Have your butcher freshly grind the meat for you. Or, cut the meat into ½-inch cubes . Put the cubes into one of the marinades (p.44) for a few hours.

2. If using ground meat, sauté the meat in a little herb-infused olive oil or herb marinade (p.46) until well browned. If using cubes of whole meat in marinade, just sauté. Be careful not to overcrowd the meat in the pan so it will brown well.

3. Pour the meat into a colander to drain off all the excess fat. Save the fat.

4. Deglaze the pan with water, wine or stock, and add those juices to the sauce.

5. Add the meat to the sauce before the simmer.

6. Chill the fat; the meat juices will settle on the bottom. Remove the fat, discard, and add the juice to the sauce.

- **Sausages** make a hearty addition to a tomato sauce. There are many varieties, but pork, veal or chicken work best. Always sauté to a golden brown to cook off as much fat as possible. As with the meat in the Bolognese sauce, always deglaze the pan after the fat has been poured off, and add to the sauce.

- **Oranges and lemons** can add an unusual twist to tomato sauce. Both the juice of the fruit and the rind can be used. I like to scrape the rind off using a fine grater. Be careful to remove only the outermost layer of the rind, avoiding the white pith, which will be bitter. Squeeze the fruit and strain the juice to avoid adding pits to the sauce. For a quart of sauce, one lemon or two oranges should lend a subtle flavor.

This sauce is particularly appropriate when seafood or chicken will be served with the pasta or cooked in the sauce.

More Variations:

All kinds of **shellfish** can be combined with one of the sauce recipes...Lobster, crabs, shrimp, clams, mussels, and scallops are among the shellfish which marry well with a tomato sauce. Either the basic or orange/lemon sauces are the best to use with fish. Personally, I hate finding bits of shell in my food, so I prefer to cook the shellfish separately and add to the sauce. Clams and mussels may be hiding sand inside, which could ruin the sauce. Raw clams removed from the shell are an exception.

To use **lobsters** or **crab**, drop them in boiling water to kill them. Cook 1 minute. Remove and allow to cool. Crack the shells and remove the meat. (Save the shells to make a stock for a seafood chowder or bisque.) For lobster, cut the bigger pieces into bite-size pieces. (The crab meat will already be in small pieces.). Add to the sauce and cook just long enough to finish cooking the meat.

Shrimp and **scallops** are best if sautéed in infused olive oil (p.46) or with one of the herb marinades (p.44). When using a marinade, and if time permits, let them marinate for a few hours. Sauté until the outside is brown, but the center a bit raw. Finish cooking in the tomato sauce. Pour off the oil and deglaze the pan with white wine or vermouth and add to the sauce.

As for **mussels**, some cooks add them directly to the sauce. I prefer to steam them open first, then remove them from their shells, thus making sure that no bits of grit or shell wind up in the finished sauce.

1. Scrub the mussels well to remove any outside grit.

2. Place them in a pan with a lid and add white wine or water, half a cup per quart of mussels. Place on high heat and allow to cook, stirring them from time to time until the shells open.

3. Pour the mussels into a colander and strain all the liquid through a chinoise strainer or several layers of cheese cloth. The liquid may be used for a fish soup or reduced by $2/3$ and added to the tomato sauce.

4. Remove the mussels from their shells, trim any "beard," and add the mussels to the sauce after it has been simmered. Just heat through.

Clams, like mussels, may be added whole to the tomato sauce, but for the same reasons I prefer to remove the meat first. You may steam them open or use the meat raw. Clams, unlike mussels, are easy to remove from their shells. To steam, follow the mussel recipe.

Raw clams may be rough-chopped and added to the sauce. Strain the clam juice as for the mussel juice, reduce by $2/3$, and add to the sauce or save for a fish soup.

Shellfish go through several changes of texture depending on how long they are cooked. If they are cooked quickly, they remain tender and have a pleasantly chewy texture. When overcooked, they become tough and unpleasant to eat. But if you keep cooking them, they will become tender again, with a softer texture. Keep this in mind when making a shellfish sauce. If you overcook in the initial stage, don't despair. Allow the fish to simmer in the tomato sauce for half hour to 1 hour and it will transform to a tender bite again. If available, add a little lemon thyme; it's like regular thyme with a citrus note—delicious—and it adds an extra note of flavor to the sauce.

- Heavy cream adds an intense richness to tomato sauce. If you are not counting calories, add ½ to 1 cup per quart of sauce.

All the variations should be seen as guidelines for you to create your own special sauce de la maison! You can combine multiple ingredients to create rich, flavorful sauces. The sauces can be used on pasta, rice, potatoes, or other grains, or as a topping for meat or fish.

Putanesca Tomato Sauce

1. Salt-packed capers have the best flavor. To use them, soak in cold water for 10 minutes. Remove to a strainer and rinse under cold running water. Allow them to drain.

   If using brine cured capers, rinse them in a strainer under cold tap water and allow them to drain.

2. Salt-packed anchovies have the best flavor. To use them, soak in cold water for ten minutes. Filet the anchovies carefully, removing the bones. Rinse them under cold running tap water.

   If using oil-packed anchovies, drain the oil (you can save it for a salad dressing). Pick over the filets to remove any bones.

3. You must use a good quality oil or brine-cured olives for this recipe. The popular canned variety have a mushy texture and no flavor; they have no place in a serious kitchen. If you cannot find olives pitted, lay them on your cutting board and slap them with the side of a chef's knife or cleaver. Remove the pits and rough-chop the olives.

4. Add all the ingredients to the basic tomato sauce and simmer for 10 minutes. If possible, make the sauce a day ahead to allow the flavors to marry.

tip

these sauces will tend to be thinner than those made from long-simmered, canned tomato purée. So if you use them for pasta, try this trick.

Cook the pasta until it is about 90% done. Drain and toss with the sauce.

Finish cooking.

The pasta will absorb the extra water in the sauce and will be that much more delicious.

If using sautéed seafood in your sauce, I would advise adding it when the pasta is almost to the desired texture to avoid overcooking the seafood.

Ingredients

¼ cup capers, salt-packed or brine cured

2 salt-packed whole anchovies, or 1 can olive oil-packed anchovies, or 1 Tablespoon anchovy paste, more or less to taste.

½ cup pitted, oil or brine-cured black olives, rough chopped

1 cup diced roasted pepper building block

½ cup roasted garlic purée building block

1-2 teaspoons red pepper flakes.

Pepper sauce

Roasted peppers make an intensely flavored sauce—a little goes a long way. Making a pepper sauce is very easy once you have the roasted peppers building block on hand. There are two types of sauces—a puréed sauce, which is creamy and smooth, and a rough-chopped sauce, where small pieces of peppers are apparent. There are many possible flavor enhancers you may add that will result in delicious variations.

Ingredients

1 cup roasted peppers building block (p.25) together with the pepper nectar.

One tablespoon roasted garlic building block (p.19) or more to taste

1 tablespoon extra virgin or herb-infused olive oil (p.46)

salt and pepper to taste

Basic purée of pepper sauce.

Put the roasted peppers and their nectar into a food processor bowl with the garlic and olive oil. Process until very smooth. Be sure to scrape down the bowl.

Voilà! You have a pepper sauce.

Variations to make sauce more complex:

• Let's look at the herbs that can complement the sauce. If you are using our homemade thyme, rosemary, and bay leaf infused oil (p.47), those flavors will be present. So a fresh green herb will be very welcome. Both **basil** and **flat leaf parsley** will add an herbal freshness to the sauce. A tablespoon of basil purée building block or ¼ cup finely chopped basil or parsley—or better yet both—will work well. Either should be added at the last minute. If you like a spicey sauce, you can increase the heat with **red pepper flakes**. Use one teaspoon to one tablespoon of flakes, depending on how many alarms you desire.

• Cooked **onions** will be another welcome addition. ½ cup of well cooked chopped onions can be added to the purée step.

• **Leeks** love peppers and the feeling is mutual! They can be added to the purée step or, as I prefer, finely chopped leeks can be stirred into the sauce after you have puréed it. They will add an interesting texture and they look great. A half cup would work well.

• Did someone say champignons or funghi? Go for it! Sautéed **mushrooms** will be right at home in the sauce. You can purée them into the sauce or, as I prefer, stir them in so you have a more interesting texture. One cup is about right. For a different texture, you can use the mushroom duxelles building block (p.29).

- **Black olives** can be added for their earthy taste. Use good quality oil- or brine-cured olives, not the pitted, canned variety, which are sorely lacking in flavor. Lay the olives on a cutting board and crack them with the flat side of a chef's knife. Remove the pits. Rough-chop them and stir them into the sauce once you have puréed it. Since olives can be salty, adjust the salt accordingly.

- A little dry **white wine** or **vermouth** is a welcome addition. You want just a whisper, not a shout, so $1/2$ cup or so will do. Another possibility is a quick trip to Spain for a little **dry sherry**—one or two tablespoons *por favor*. Either wine can be added before or after the puréeing process.

- If you are using the sauce with meat or fish, a little red or white wine vinegar, balsamic **vinegar**, or **lemon juice** will add more depth to the sauce. Use 1 tablespoon of balsamic vinegar or lemon juice, or 1 teaspoon of red wine vinegar.

- **Capers** and **anchovies** are strong flavors—just a touch should be added. You can use canned salted **anchovies** or anchovy paste. Capers or anchovy paste are especially helpful if the sauce will be used for meat or fish. One tablespoon of capers, several anchovy filets, or a teaspoon of anchovy paste will do it. Just add the anchovy paste during the puréeing process, or stir the capers into the sauce after the purée process. The sauce becomes a red pepper putanesca with the addition of some **red pepper flakes**; try $1/2$ teaspoon. Add more if more heat is desired.

- **Heavy cream** makes for a very rich sauce and is quite delicious. For each quart of sauce, add between a few tablespoons and $1/2$ cup of sauce.

Rough Pepper Sauce

To make a rough pepper sauce, either rough-chop the peppers by hand or pulse them in a food processor. You may use any of the flavorings outlined for the puréed sauce. Another possibility is to combine both methods, adding rough-chopped peppers to the purée. This can be very effective if you use different colored peppers, for example, a red pepper purée with a rough yellow or orange pepper added for texture and color contrast.

Pesto Sauce

Traditionally, pesto sauce is made with basil, pine nuts, raw garlic, Parmesan cheese, olive oil, salt and pepper. I like to follow tradition with two changes. Instead of raw garlic I like to use roasted garlic. I find raw garlic can be hard to digest; it causes heartburn for many people. Second, I lightly toast the pinenuts, which deepens their flavor.

Pesto is not the place to compromise on olive oil; use the finest quality extra virgin olive oil you can afford. I recommend a ripe, dark green, fruity oil. Only use the best Reggiano Parmesan. Everything else is merely chopped formaggio!

Pesto Sauce

Ingredients

2 cups tightly packed basil leaves, washed and dried

$1/2$ cup flat leaf parsley (optional, but adds an interesting note)

$1/2$ cup olive oil

$1/2$ cup lightly toasted pine nuts

$1/3$ cup roasted garlic building block

$1/2$ cup grated Parmesan cheese

$1/2$ teaspoon fresh ground pepper

$1/2$ teaspoon fine sea salt

1. In a food processor purée all the ingredients until they form a smooth paste. Scrape down the bowl once during the process to dislodge any bits on the sides.

Walnuts may be substituted for pine nuts, but be sure to toast them.

Toasting walnuts

1. Toast the walnuts in the oven or microwave. In a conventional oven, pre-heat to 350°, then place the nuts in a single layer on a sheet pan. Roast them for 5-8 minutes, stirring once or twice for even baking, until the nuts darken and the skin begins to flake.

If you prefer to microwave, lay the walnuts in a single layer in an appropriate microwave pan. Zap them in 30 second intervals, shaking them each time, until they they have darkened and the skin begins to flake.

2. Rub the walnuts in a clean dish towel to remove the skins, which can impart a bitter taste. It's not necessary to remove all the skins.

You can store the pesto in the refrigerator, covered with olive oil. It will keep well for a week in the fridge, or for months in the freezer.

Garlic Sauce

O ne of the simplest sauces to serve with pasta, garlic sauce is traditionally prepared by sautéing garlic in olive oil. I prefer to make it with roasted garlic purée.

Garlic Sauce

Whisk all the ingredients together until well mixed. Toss with hot pasta, roasted or poached fish, chicken, or steamed or grilled vegetables.

Using our building blocks and other additions, we can make the garlic sauce even more delicious...

Ingredients

$^{1}/_{2}$ cup extra virgin olive oil

$^{1}/_{4}$ cup garlic purée building block (p.19)

$^{1}/_{2}$ teaspoon fresh-ground pepper

$^{1}/_{4}$ teaspoon sea salt

Variations:

- For a deeper flavor, substitute **herb infused olive oil** for the extra virgin oil.

- For a spicy garlic sauce add $^{1}/_{2}$ to 1 teaspoon **red pepper flakes** to the mixture before or after puréeing.

- **Italian parsley** or **basil** added during the purée step is welcome. Use the fresh leaves or the basil purée building block. (p.46) You may decrease the oil by $^{1}/_{4}$ cup.

- Diced concasse **tomatoes** (p.11) or diced roasted **peppers** (p.25), lightly warmed, will add a wonderful color and flavor. Fold into sauce after the purée step. Use $^{1}/_{2}$ cup.

- **Mushrooms** and **garlic** make a natural combination. Just add warm mushrooms—either the sliced or duxelle building block—to the sauce after the purée step.(p.29) Use $^{1}/_{2}$ cup.

- **Leeks** will lend their distinctive flavor and creamy texture to the garlic sauce.(p.23) You can purée them with the garlic or add them afterwards. Use $^{1}/_{2}$ cup.

- Many of our **bean** building blocks will add their nutty flavor and texture to the sauce. Chick peas work very well, as will lentils.(p.37) They should be warmed and folded into the sauce

- Blanched green beans, broccoli, zucchini, or peas add a wonderful color, flavor, and texture.

As with most recipes in the book these should be used as guidelines or points of departure. Mix and match to create your own favorite combinations.

Salads, Dips, and Dressings

It's a snap to create great salads, dips, and dressings with the right building blocks in your pantry.

Bean Salads

When beans have been cooked (p.35) and are still warm, they are at their most receptive to becoming a delicious bean salad. The basic recipe is to toss the warm beans with extra-virgin olive oil and some type of vinegar.

Here is the entire recipe. The rest is commentary...

1. For each cup of warm beans toss 3 tablespoons of oil and 1-2 teaspoons or more of vinegar. (Traditional Tuscan bean salad uses no vinegar at all. It's a matter of taste.) Add salt and pepper to taste.

One of my favorite vinegars for bean salad is good quality balsamic vinegar. You could also use one of our herb-infused red wine vinegars, white wine vinegars, or sherry wine vinegars, or a combination of them (p.48). I also like to add a spritz of fresh-squeezed lemon juice. Wine and sherry vinegars are stronger than balsamic, so if you use balsamic, you can use more. Remember, you want the vinegar to whisper, not shout!

Walnut oil or hazelnut oil provides an interesting change of pace from olive. You may also try different combinations of the various oils and vinegars.

To make the bean salad extra special add a teaspoon of fresh thyme leaves and a tablespoon of garlic purée (p.19). Yes, it's tedious to pick those tiny little thyme leaves, but there is no substitute. As a garnish, chopped Italian parsley or basil can lend their wonderful color and flavor. Possible additions are diced, roasted peppers or pepper purée, leeks, onions, or shallots that have been slow cooked, diced concasse tomatoes, or—a personal favorite—lightly toasted pine nuts and sautéed portobello mushrooms with a dusting of Parmesan cheese—yum!

Bean Salad purées

Beans are wonderful whole, but they can also be transformed into a smooth purée to serve as a bed for vegetables, chicken, pork, beef, lamb, or fish. Or, bean purées can become wonderful dips for chips, bread, or crackers. Bean purées also make excellent low-fat sandwich spreads.

Humous Ingredients

- **1 cup chickpea building block, drained (p.37)**
- **¹/₃ cup tahini (sesame seed paste). Use roasted tahini paste if available.**
- **¹/₄ cup boiling water or bean liquid, if needed**
- **1 tablespoon garlic purée building block (p.19), or more to taste**
- **¹/₂ teaspoon ground cumin**
- **¹/₄ teaspoon ground coriander seed**
- **¹/₃ cup extra virgin olive oil, or one of the herb-infused oils**
- **¹/₃ cup fresh squeezed lemon juice**
- **¹/₄ cup toasted sesame seeds (optional)**
- **¹/₂ teaspoon fresh ground black pepper**
- **¹/₂ teaspoon sea salt**

Any of the above bean salads can be puréed and used for these purposes.

The best known bean salad purée is chickpea purée, better known as humous. This variation on the traditional recipe tastes better than any version you can find in a deli.

Humous

1. In a food processor, purée the beans to a paste.
2. Add the tahini. Purée to blend.
3. Add the remaining ingredients except the toasted sesame seeds. Purée to blend well. You may add up to ¹/₄ cup boiling water or bean liquid, a little at a time, if the mixture is too thick. Taste and adjust the salt and pepper.
4. Pulse in the sesame seeds.
5. Serve with chopped flat leaf parsley.

Lentil Salad

For each cup of cooked lentils add some or all of the ingredients according to your taste.

Toss together. Enjoy with some crisp bread.

¼ cup infused olive oil

2-3 tablespoons pitted black olives (see p.59)

½ cup feta or other goat cheese, cut into small pieces

½ cup of one of the following: rough-chopped roasted pepper (p.25), oven-dried plum tomato (p.15), or concasse tomato (p.11)

1-2 teaspoons capers (see p.59)

2 teaspoons fresh-squeezed lemon juice

chopped Italian parsley

½ teaspoon fresh-ground pepper

a pinch of salt if desired remember—capers, olives, and goat cheese can already be salty)

With eggplant purée building block on hand, (p.35) it's a snap to whip up some baba ganoush, also known as eggplant caviar.

Baba Ganoush

Purée ingredients together in a blender or food processor.

Baba Ganoush Ingredients

1 cup eggplant purée

2 tablespoons garlic purée

¼ cup extra-virgin olive oil. Thyme- and rosemary-infused olive oil works very well here (p.45).

2 tablespoons lemon juice

¼ cup tightly packed parsley

1-3 tablespoons tahini, preferably toasted sesame paste (optional)

1 teaspoon fresh-ground pepper

½ teaspoon sea salt

Melitzano Ingredients

¹/₂ cup walnuts

1 cup roasted eggplant
building block (p.35)

¹/₄ cup roasted garlic purée
building block (p.19)

¹/₂ cup extra virgin olive oil
or an infused oil (p.45)

1 tablespoon white wine
(optional)

1 tablespoon lemon juice or
vinegar infused with fresh
herbs (p.48)

¹/₂ teaspoon dried oregano or
1 teaspoon fresh

optionally, ¹/₄ cup pitted
Kalamata olives

optionally, ¹/₄ cup concasse,
oven roasted or dried tomatoes (pp.11, 14, 15)

¹/₂ teaspoon pepper

¹/₂ teaspoon salt

Melitzano Salata

A Greek version of eggplant dip

1. Toast the walnuts (see sidebar on toasting walnuts, p.62).

2. Put all ingredients into a food processor and process until smooth.

3. Optionally fold the olives or tomatoes, or both, into the eggplant purée.

4. Taste and adjust salt and pepper.

5. Blend all the ingredients together and let rest for 24 hours, ideally, or for at least a few hours, so the flavors can marry. Remember, the salad should always be served at room temperature so all the flavor and texture of the salad is at its peak.

6. I sometimes like to add olives. The best to use are the tiny Niçoise olives or one of the black cured olives. When using them, I like to crack them with the flat of a chef knife. Remove the pits or not? Depends who is coming to dine. Just be sure to warn your guests! The standard black American canned olives are of no use here—they're so tasteless and soggy, I'm yawning.

Roasted Pepper Salad

Roasted pepper salads are very popular. There are many variations of this salad. The basic recipe follows.

This pepper salad stands fine on its own, but you can serve it with a cheese for a more substantial dish. Serve it over slices of fresh mozzarella cheese, especially creamy buffalo-milk mozzarella. The small balls of mozzarella known as *bocconcini* go well with pepper salad also. Fresh creamy goat cheese works very well with pepper salad. Another cheese which works well is Reggiano Parmesan; use a potato peeler to slice thin "shards" of cheese and layer over the top of the pepper salad.

For garnish, lightly toasted pine nuts or sesame seeds and shredded fresh basil or chopped parsley finish the plate, adding visual appeal as well as flavor. Another possible garnish is fresh oregano leaves. Note that all nuts and seeds keep well in the freezer. Like vegetable oils, nut oils will turn rancid if kept in too warm a place.

Roasted Pepper Salad Ingredients

- 1 cup roasted peppers (p.25), drained of juice, in large pieces or cut into strips

- 2 teaspoons garlic purée

- 1 tablespoon fresh-squeezed lemon juice

- 1/4 cup extra-virgin olive oil, or one of the herb-infused oils (p.46)

- 1-2 tablespoon capers. As always, I prefer the salt-packed capers (see Putanesca sauce, p.59), but capers packed in brine also work well. Rinse with water and pat dry before using.

- 1 teaspoon anchovy paste, or 1 can anchovies packed in olive oil, or several salt packed anchovies. (The differences among them are discussed in the Putanesca sauce recipe, p.59.)

- 1 teaspoon fresh-ground pepper

Purées Ingredients

1 cup roasted peppers (p.25), drained of juice

¼ cup cooked onions, shallots, or—best of all— leeks (pp.21, 23)

1 tablespoon roasted garlic purée (p.19) or more to taste

¼ cup olive oil

2 teaspoons lemon juice

2 teaspoons balsamic vinegar (this really complements the natural sweetness of the peppers)

½ teaspoon fresh-ground pepper

½ teaspoon fine sea salt

Skordaliais Ingredients

1 cup potato purée building block. (p.32) Try a 50/50 mix of Yukon gold and Idaho.

¼ cup roasted garlic building block (p.19)

½ cup extra virgin olive oil, or one of the infused oils (p.46)

2 tablespoons fresh squeezed lemon juice

1 tablespoon red wine vinegar or herb-infused red wine vinegar (p.48)

optionally, ½ cup roasted walnuts, chopped fine

Roasted Pepper purées

Another wonderful treatment of roasted peppers is to make them into a dip or spread. It is very simple with a blender or food processor.

1. Put all the ingredients together and purée in blender or food processor. Adjust salt and pepper to taste.

Voilà. that's all there is to it! Use the roasted pepper purée as a dip for raw vegetables, or a sandwich spread; try it with some crusty bread and thinly sliced Prosciutto de Parma, and a drizzle of basil oil or some fresh basil leaves, yummy!

This purée can also be made with oven dried tomatoes instead of pepper or in a combination.

Skordaliais

Important: *never* use a food processor to make this dish! The action of the blade will develop the starch in the potatoes, resulting in a rubbery mess.

1. If you include the walnuts, roasting them will give them a much better taste. See "How to roast walnuts," p.62.
2. Put the potato purée into a bowl with all the ingredients. Mix and blend together into a smooth paste. A wooden spoon works well for this task.

While walnuts are traditionally used in Greece, I have had delicious success with toasted almonds or pine nuts.

Caramelized Onion Spread

Caramelized onions (p.21) make a wonderful spread, which is simplicity itself to make. Just purée some caramelized onions in a blender or food processor and you have a creamy spread. Sometimes I like to add a little balsamic vinegar to really gild the onion! Just a teaspoon or two per cup of onion will sharpen the natural sweetness of the onions.

Salad Dressings

The basic vinaigrette is traditionally made with vinegar or citrus juice, paired with a vegetable oil.

You can choose among red or white wine vinegar, balsamic vinegar, or sherry wine vinegar. It is very important to use the best quality vinegar. Avoid the bulk-produced vinegars and seek out those aged in oak casks. There is so much cheap and poor quality balsamic vinegar flooding the market; seek out the real thing, aged in oak casks at least 5 years or more, as your pocketbook allows.

The best vegetable oil for salad dressing is extra-virgin olive oil. Sometimes it's nice to vary the oil by using walnut oil. There is no substitute for fresh, earthy, oils with a good flavor. Of course, for olive oil look for an extra virgin oil with a rich olive flavor. The best walnut oils are usually imported from France. Buy it in small quantities, as a little goes a long way.

I alway keep my oils in the refrigerator so they won't become dull or rancid. Refrigerated oils coagulate but melt very quickly when at room temperature. If you're impatient, you can run some hot water on the bottle to speed the flow. I don't know how many times I've arrived at a client's home to find a very expensive bottle of oil spoiled from sitting in a warm cupboard. I always keep a spare bottle in my bag!

All the vinaigrettes shown below will dress a selection of salad greens or raw vegetables. Fresh fruits, such as ripe peaches, pears, figs, mangoes, papayas, fresh orange or grapefruit sections, blueberries, raspberries, strawberries, or fuji persimmons can enhance your salads. Delicious!

Vinaigrette Ingredients

- 1 tablespoon of one of the above vinegars or infused vinegar building block (p.48)

- a pinch of salt and fresh-ground pepper

- $1/2$ teaspoon mustard (the French usually include it; the Italians don't. It's a matter of taste—try it both ways, but use good quality mustard.)

- 3 tablespoons olive oil, extra virgin or one of the infused olive oils

The basic recipe for a vinaigrette

1 part vinegar to 3 parts oil. This is a good point of departure. You can always adjust the ingredients to suit your own taste. You may want to use vinegar or oil that has been infused with fresh herbs to make them even more flavorful.

Vinaigrette will keep refrigerated for a week but the flavor begins to fade, so I prefer to make a fresh batch each time. Think about how much you need—a little goes a long way. I find people often make much more that they need, and the ingredients can be expensive if you are using top quality oils and vinegars. So let's explore some recipes using tablespoons instead of cups!

Red, white, sherry wine, or balsamic vinaigrette

The basic idea is to mix the vinegar and spices first, so the salt dissolves, and add the oil afterwards.

1. Vinegar step. Mix vinegar, salt, pepper and mustard together. Either shake in a small jar or whisk in a small bowl to blend well. (You can also use a blender)

2. Oil step. Add oil to jar and shake well or whisk oil into the bowl, or zap in blender with the vinegar mixture.

That's it! There are many ways to customize this basic recipe to your taste.

Variations:

Garlic vinaigrette

To the basic vinaigrette recipe add 1 teaspoon (or more to taste) of garlic purée building block. Add the garlic purée after the vinegar step, but before the oil step. A blender makes this quick work.

Garlic-Parmesan vinaigrette

Add a tablespoon of grated Parmesan cheese with the garlic after the vinegar step. Use a bit less salt, as Parmesan has salt in it—you don't want the salt to overwhelm the flavor.

Garlic-Roasted Pepper vinaigrette (1)

Add 1 tablespoon of puréed or chopped roasted pepper building block (p.25) along with the garlic after the vinegar step. A bit of anchovy paste adds a little zing—$1/2$ teaspoon is about right. Since anchovy paste is salty, reduce the amount of salt in the basic recipe.

Garlic-Roasted Pepper vinaigrette (2)

Add 1 tablespoon of puréed or finely chopped roasted pepper building block (p.24) along with the garlic after the vinegar step. For this variation, use sherry wine vinegar. Complement with flat leaf Italian parsley, added after the vinegar step.

Garlic-Tomato Vinaigrette

Add a few oven-dried tomatoes, either puréed or finely chopped, with the garlic after the vinegar step. I like using balsamic vinegar and lemon juice in a 2 to 1 ratio for this vinaigrette. Basil purée or basil oil, combined in a 1 to 1 ratio with olive oil, will complement the garlic-tomato flavors.

Leek vinaigrette

Add $1/4$ cup of leek building block (p.23) after the vinegar step. If you use a blender, the leek purée will give the vinaigrette a smooth creamy texture.

Caramelized Onion vinaigrette

Like leeks, caramelized onions (p.21) will add a creamy texture to the vinaigrette. Add them after the vinegar step. Try substituting walnut oil for the olive oil in this recipe.

Basil vinaigrette

Instead of olive oil, use basil oil (p.46) or a blend of the two. A teaspoon of garlic makes basil vinaigrette even better. For those of you who love pesto sauce, you can make this a pesto vinaigrette by adding 2 teaspoons of garlic, 1 tablespoon of Parmesan cheese, and 1 tablespoon of toasted pine nuts. Zap in a blender.

Citrus vinaigrette

Lemon and orange rind add flavor interest to vinaigrette. Add a teaspoon of grated lemon or orange rind to the basic vinaigrette after the vinegar step. You may also want to substitute fresh squeezed lemon juice for half the vinegar in the recipe. A bit of garlic is welcome here—1 teaspoon works well.

Vinaigrette with body

If you like more "body" in your vinaigrette, you may add half a hard-boiled egg yolk after the vinegar step to any of the above variations. A blender will make for a smooth emulsion. Avoid using raw yolks, since salmonella may be lurking. A case of food poisoning could really ruin your day!

Soup

The most important thing to remember is great soups need great stocks as their foundation. With a great stock you are almost assured a very memorable soup unless you burn it. I prefer to make most soups with chicken or vegetable stocks, but of course it is really a matter of taste. When you start with a vibrant, richly flavored stock, adding other ingredients will only make it better.

Soups should be served in warm, attractive bowls with a soup spoon that possesses a good sized bowl and some heft. It will make eating the soup that much more of a pleasure.

Good, crusty bread is a must to accompany the soup. Alternatively, use one of the "improved" bread ideas from the Bruschetta and Pizza chapter, (p.112). Nothing warms the soul like a steaming bowl of great soup.

Tomato soups

There are countless types of tomato soup; once you know how to make the basic soup, you can go experiment with one of the variations.

Basic Tomato Soup

1. Bring the stock and tomato purée or juice to a boil. Reduce to a simmer.

2. Whisk in the onion, garlic purée, salt and pepper, and the diced tomato. Simmer for $1/2$ hour.

3. Taste for seasonings.

4. Garnish with fresh chopped Italian parsley or chopped chives, and drizzle with your best extra virgin olive oil or basil-infused oil.

   If you are a fan of tarragon or chervil, 1-2 teaspoons finely chopped and sprinkled over the soup is delightful.

Tomato-beef soup is one exception to my stock preference—this is one soup I find works well with beef stock. But I prefer to eat it as is and not add any of the many ingredients outlined in the following recipes. Chopped chives, parsley or basil are all it needs.

Tomato-Basil Soup

1. After the 3rd step in the Basic Tomato Soup recipe, whisk in $1/2$ cup chopped basil.

2. No need to cook the soup any longer. Serve in warm soup bowls.

3. Some interesting garnishes: drizzle with extra virgin olive oil, a sprinkle of chopped toasted pinenuts, grated Reggiano Parmesan cheese and finely chopped Italian parsley.

Ingredients

2 cups chicken stock, beef stock, or vegetable stock

1 cup tomato purée, or 3 cups tomato juice reduced to 1 cup

$1/4$ cup sautéed onions

2-3 tablespoons roasted garlic purée

1 teaspoon fresh picked thyme leaves (no stems need apply)

$1/2$ teaspoon salt and fresh ground pepper

(optional) $1/2$ -1 cup diced concasse tomato (p.11)

Tomato-Arugula Soup

1. Wash the arugula very well to remove any bits of dirt or sand. Drain well. Remove any tough stems.

2. Gather the arugula into a stack of leaves and shred into $\frac{1}{4}$-inch pieces. 1 cup per recipe will work well—a little more or less is fine. There is no exact amount.

3. Stir into the Basic Tomato Soup after step 3 in the basic recipe

4. Any of the garnishes for Tomato-Basil Soup will work here. Try a dusting of lightly roasted sesame seeds.

Tomato-Spinach Soup

1. Wash the spinach well to remove any dirt and sand. Drain well. Remove any tough stems.

2. Stack the leaves and shred into $\frac{1}{4}$-inch slices.

3. Stir into Basic Tomato Soup after step 3 of the basic recipe.

4. Garnish with any of the ideas for Tomato Basil Soup.

I like to serve this soup with a lemon wedge on the side, and a drizzle of basil oil. (p.46.)

Tomato-Escarole Soup

1. Wash the escarole very well (it can be very sandy). Rip or chop into bite-sized pieces.

2. Add to the soup and simmer until tender, about 45 minutes.

3. White beans are a wonderful addition, and grated Parmesan is a must! A few toasted pine nuts will put it over the top.

Tomato-Leek Soup

1. Add 1 cup of leek building block (p.23) to the Basic Tomato Soup recipe.

2. Garnish with chives.

Tomato-Onion Soup

1. Add 1 cup of caramelized onion building block. (p.21)
2. Garnish with parsley or chives.

Tomato-Zucchini Soup

1. Scrub the zucchini and either shred or cut into very tiny dice (1/8-inch cubes).
2. Sprinkle with fine sea salt (1 teaspoon per cup of zucchini) and mix.
3. Let the zucchini stand for 20 minutes in a colander. Drain and squeeze out excess moisture from the zucchini, then press between paper towels. This will give the zucchini a more interesting texture
4. Lightly sauté in a little olive oil for 5 minutes. Do not overcook—we want it to have a bit of crunch.
5. Stir into the warm Basic Tomato Soup and serve
6. Any of the garnishes mentioned will work well here also. My favorite garnishes for this dish are goat cheese and Parmesan bruschette. (p.112)

Tomato-Cucumber Soup

This soup works well cold or hot. I prefer the long English cucumbers for this soup. Select firm, non-bruised specimens.

1. Peel and seed the cucumber.
2. Dice the cucumber into tiny pieces—1/8-inch cubes would be ideal. Or if that is too much work, pulse the cucumbers in a food processor to a rough chop—you want small pieces, not a purée.
3. Add to the Basic Tomato Soup after step 3 and simmer for 5 minutes.
4. Serve hot or cold. Basil, Italian parsley or tarragon are herbs that will complement the soup. You might consider fresh dill, which has a special affinity for cucumbers.

Tomato-Bean or Tomato-Lentil Soup

1. To the Basic Tomato Soup add an extra $1/4$ cup of garlic purée and 1 cup of cooked beans or lentils (p.37). While any kind of beans will work well, I really love white beans for this soup. $1/2$ to 1 cup of sautéed leeks is a real plus. Tomatoes, beans, and leeks make a great trio.

2. Simmer together for 10 minutes.

3. Any of the herb garnishes mentioned will work well here, especially parsley and basil.

I love grated Parmesan cheese in this soup.

Finely sliced green beans, especially the thin haricots verts, make an interesting color contrast when tossed into the soup. To incorporate green beans into this soup, slice them into $1/8$-inch pieces, blanch in boiling, lightly salted water (one minute only), refresh in cold water, add to the hot soup, and simmer for just 1 minute to re-heat before serving. Don't overcook or they will loose their crunch..

Tomato with Roasted Eggplant Soup

1. To the Basic Tomato Soup recipe add 1 cup of roasted eggplant purée. I like to increase the garlic by $1/4$ cup.

2. A garnish of chopped parsley and a squeeze of lemon juice will add a wonderful zip to the soup. Another wonderful addition is a handful of mozzarella cheese, regular or smoked, diced into tiny cubes—just scatter the cheese into the soup after it has been served in bowls.

3. A pinch of Parmesan cheese as garnish will make it extra special.

4. A drizzle of basil oil and a sprinkle of chopped parsley and—mama mia—you've made liquid eggplant Parmesan!

Tomato and Mushroom Soup

1. To the Basic Tomato Soup add 1 cup of sliced or diced mushroom building block (p.29) or mushroom duxelle (p.30). While any of the mushrooms from the mushroom chapter will work well, I really love diced portobello in this recipe.

2. Add ½ cup of dry vermouth or dry sherry—sherry is especially appropriate here.

3. Simmer together for 15 minutes.

4. Leeks are a wonderful addition to this soup, either as a dice or a purée. Add ½ cup of either.

5. Garnish with any of the fresh green herbs. A little Parmesan cheese is also a tasty addition, or serve with Parmesan bruschetta. (p.112)

Tomato-Orange Soup

Tomato and orange combine to create a taste made in heaven! They complement each other amazingly well. This is one of my all time favorite soups!

1. To the Basic Tomato Soup add the grated rind of two oranges. Use a fine grater and remember to turn the orange frequently, taking off only the orange outer skin while avoiding the bitter white pith underneath. Simmer in the soup for 15 minutes.

2. Squeeze the juice from the oranges, strain to remove any seeds, add to the soup, and simmer for 5 minutes.

3. Garnish with a slice of fresh orange, and a chopped green herb such as parsley, basil, tarragon, chervil, or chives.

For a more interesting texture you can add ½ cup of diced carrots. They should be very small cubes, sautéed in olive oil just enough to lose their "raw" taste but still with a good "bite."

Tomato-Vegetable Soup

1. To the Basic Tomato Soup recipe, add a mixture of your favorite green and root vegetables. The season should dictate which vegetables you use.

1a. For root vegetables, such as potatoes, carrots, or parsnips, dice them into $1/4$-inch cubes or pulse-chop them in the food processor into small pieces, sauté for 5 minutes in a bit of olive oil, then add to the soup and simmer.

1b. For green vegetables such as green beans, celery, peas, broccoli florettes, squash, or spinach, blanch them in boiling, salted water for one minute, refresh them in cold water to lock in their vibrant green color, then cut them into fine pieces, add them to the soup, and cook for just one minute to heat through. The vegetables should still have some crunch. You may want to add some pasta to the soup. You can use pastina noodles or any of the smaller shapes.

2. Garnish with Reggiano Parmesan cheese and basil-infused oil (p.46).

Tomato-Pepper Soup

1. To the Basic Tomato Soup, add 1 cup of diced or puréed roasted pepper building block (p.25). As always, when I think of peppers, I think leeks, and $1/2$ cup of leek building block (p.23) would make this soup extra special.

2. Garnish with basil oil (p.46)

Garlic Soups

Garlic Soups are very simple and delicious — just the ticket for garlic lovers.

Basic Garlic Soup

1. To chicken stock or vegetable stock add garlic purée (p.19).

That is the entire recipe—what could be simpler? I like to use a heaping $1/2$ cup of garlic purée for each quart of stock. You may increase or decrease this amount according to your taste. And while it is delicious as is, you may add one or more of the following as a garnish for additional flavor and complexity...

- **Diced concasse.** Just stir the tomato (p.11) into the simmering soup prior to serving. The pieces of tomato look wonderful and taste great. Garnish with basil, parsley, or chives, or a drizzle of basil-infused oil.

- **Roasted peppers.** Add a confetti of finely diced peppers—red, yellow, orange or green (p.25). Just stir into the hot soup and simmer for 1 minute.

  Another way to make a pepper-garlic soup is to purée the peppers. Fill a squirt bottle like the kind used to serve ketchup or mustard, and squirt pepper purée over the soup in a zig-zag or spiral pattern. This will look and taste great.

- **Basil** or **parsley** would be an excellent garnish, as would a drizzle of basil-infused oil. (p.46)

- **Mushroom.** Add 1 cup of diced or sliced mushroom building block (p.28) or mushroom duxelles (p.29) and $1/2$ cup of sautéed onions, shallots or leeks.

- **Roasted Eggplant.** Add 1 cup of purée per quart of stock, or more to taste. I like to add fresh-squeezed lemon juice (approximately 1 tablespoon).

- A garnish of **chopped parsley** and a drizzle of **olive oil** and voilà! Parmesan bruschetta work wonderfully here.

- **Cooked beans.** Beans can be added to the garlic soup to create a wonderful garlic bean soup. Just add $1/2$ to 2 cups cooked beans per quart, depending on how beany you want the soup. You may prefer to purée some of the beans. Serve with Goat Cheese Bruschetta with Sesame Seeds (p.112).

Garlic with Leek or Onion Soup

Add 1 cup cooked leek or onion building block (pp.21, 23) or a combination to the soup. Garnish with chopped chives.

Garlic-Potato Soup

Add 1 cup of potato purée (p.32) and a teaspoon of thyme leaves to the soup. Garlic chives make a great garnish.

Optionally, add $1/2$ cup of grated cheese to create a Garlic-Potato-Cheese soup. Parmesan or cheddar work well.

Garlic-Lemon Soup

1. To the Basic Garlic Soup, add 1-2 Tablespoons of fresh squeezed lemon juice.
2. Flat-leafed parsley and a drizzle of olive oil for garnish complete the picture.

Garlic with Greens Soup

Spinach or arugula can be added to the Basic Garlic Soup. Either should be well washed and then chopped or torn into bite-sized pieces. Just add to the simmering soup until they wilt. The soup is now ready to serve. Serve with a grated Parmesan cheese.

Garlic with Green Herbs Soup

To the Basic Garlic Soup, add 1 cup of a combination of the following green herbs: basil, flat-leaf parsley, chives, chervil, and tarragon. Rough-chop the herbs and stir into the simmering soup. Serve with a drizzle of olive oil. If you want to keep the herbs' vibrant color, blanch in boiling water for 45 seconds and then refresh in cold water before adding to soup.

Leek Soups

Leek and Potato Soup

Leek and Potato Soup is also known as Vichysoisse when puréed. Served hot or cold, it's a classic.

1. Blend all ingredients together well in a food processor.
2. Serve hot or cold.
3. Garnish with chopped chives.

Variations:

You can add up to 1 cup of heavy cream. Just whisk into the soup. I like to serve the cream on the side in either of two ways:

• Lightly whip the heavy cream right from the container. Let each person add one, two, or three dollops to taste.

• Put some heavy cream in a "squeeze bottle," (like the kind used for ketchup or mustard). Shake until the body of the cream has thickened somewhat but is still liquid. Let each person squirt their own design into their soup bowl.

Remember, the cream should be very cold before either method is used. In any case, a shower of fresh chopped chives is almost a must.

Ingredients

1 quart rich chicken or vegetable stock (pp.39,40)

2 cups potato purée (p.32)

1 cup cooked leeks (p.37)

1 tablespoon garlic purée (p.19)

Leek and Roasted Pepper Soup

I find the marriage of leeks and peppers to be a blissful union.

1. Combine ingredients to make a great soup. You may purée either the peppers or the leeks, or neither, as you choose.
2. Add salt and pepper to taste.
3. Drizzle with basil-infused oil to garnish.

Leek and Pepper Ingredients

1 quart chicken or vegetable stock (p.39,40)

1 cup prepared leeks (p.23)

1 cup roasted peppers (p.25)

1 tablespoon garlic purée (p.19)

Leek and Bean Soup

1. Add 1 cup of prepared leeks (p.23) and 1 cup of beans—garbanzos or white beans work best (p.37)—to 1 quart of vegetable or chicken stock.

2. Serve with Parmesan bruschetta (p.112).

Squash & Pumpkin soups

Squash/Pumpkin Ingredients

1 quart chicken or vegetable stock (pp.39, 40)

2 cups pumpkin or squash purée (p.33)

1 tablespoon garlic purée (p.19)

$1/2$ cup chopped onion, leek, or shallot building block (pp.21-23)

Squash/Pumpkin Soup

Pumpkin, or any of the orange-fleshed winter squashes, makes a delicious soup. I especially love Kabocha squash because of its rich color and flavor. The basic recipe is:

1. Purée all the ingredients until smooth.

2. Simmer 15 minutes.

3. Serve with a drizzle of basil-infused oil and toasted almonds or pumpkin seeds.

Additions and Variations

• Add the rind and juice of two oranges to the soup. Remember, be careful to avoid any of the white pith. Simmer $1/2$ hour.

• Add a fine dice of lightly sautéed carrots, as we did for the Tomato Orange Soup (p.79).

• Curry powder is a popular addition to this soup. Use 1 tablespoon curry powder. You should always toast the curry powder for five minutes in a frying pan to bring out the best flavor. For a sweet reward, substitute 1 cup fresh apple juice for one cup of stock.

• For a very dramatic presentation, serve this soup in a baked pumpkin. It's very easy. Just cut off the top of a pumpkin large enough to hold the amount of soup you plan to serve. Scrape out the pumpkin, and trim the cap of any strings.

Brush the pumpkin and cap lightly with oil. Bake in a 350˚ oven until the interior flesh is a little tender and the skin has darkened. Don't overbake! It must be able to keep its shape.

• Some shredded real Cheddar cheese makes a great extra treat.

• Toasted pumpkin seeds make a great garnish.

Purée of Green Vegetable Soups

Any of the Green Vegetable Purées (p.34) makes a fine cream of vegetable soup. Just add 1-2 cups of purée to 1 quart of chicken or vegetable stock. The addition of ½ cup of onion building block and 1-2 tablespoons of garlic purée will enhance the flavor. Just simmer for 15 minutes. Serve with Parmesan or goat cheese bruschette. (p.112)

Onion Soups

When one has caramelized onions and good stock on hand, French onion soup, that perennial favorite, is just a quick simmer away from reality. The traditional soup is made with rich beef stock. It retains a well-deserved place in the classic repertoire. But there are lighter versions to consider, especially one made with chicken stock and apple juice.

The classic and lighter onion soups follow, with variations. Serve the soups with a slice of cheese toast. Gruyère cheese is traditional, but other cheeses can be used.

Classic Soup Ingredients

1 quart rich beef stock (p.41)

2 cups caramelized onions (p.21)

1-2 tablespoons good brandy or cognac (optional)

Several slices good, crusty French bread, cut into ½-inch slices. Day-old bread works well here.

Sliced or shredded Gruyère cheese to cover

Classic French Onion Soup with Beef Stock

1. Combine the stock, onions, and cognac. Bring to a boil and cook ½ hour at a steady simmer.

2. Lightly toast the French bread. Sprinkle a layer of cheese on the bread.

3. Pour the soup into an oven-proof crock or into a set of oven-proof bowls, and place the pieces of bread and cheese on top.

4. Bake in a 450° oven until the cheese has melted and browned.

If you lack an oven-proof crock or bowls, you can bake the bread and cheese in the oven, place them in soup bowls, and pour the hot soup over them. The results are not as aesthetically pleasing, but still taste wonderful.

Soup with Apples Ingredients

3 cups chicken stock (p.40)

1 cup apple juice. If you have a juicer, by all means make fresh-squeezed juice. If not, use commercial fresh juice.

2 cups caramelized onions (p.21)

1 cup apples, peeled and cut into a small dice, tossed with a tablespoon of fresh-squeezed lemon juice, and then sautéed in 2 teaspoons of butter until a light golden color is achieved.

1-2 tablespoons Calvados (apple brandy), optional

Salt and pepper to taste

Several slices good, crusty French bread, cut into ½-inch slices. Day-old bread works well here.

Sliced or shredded Gruyère cheese to cover

Onion Soup with Apples

I once tasted a delightful version of onion soup, which used chicken stock, apple juice, and calvados. I have recreated the recipe here. Use a tart, firm apple, like Granny Smith.

This soup is prepared the same way as the classic version, except that sautéed apple is added before the baking, or is simmered with the soup for 15 minutes before serving.

Variations

• As a change of pace, try using goat cheese, Parmesan, or a combination, instead of the usual Gruyère cheese.

Cream of Onion Soup

Cream of Onion is a smooth, creamy soup that can be made with either version of the onion building blocks, the basic sautéed onions or the caramelized onions. The amount of cream you add depends on your taste and the state of your waistline.

1. Put the onions and garlic in a food processor or blender with 1 cup of stock and purée until very smooth.

2. Scrape the mixture into a sauce pan.

3. Swish more chicken stock in the food processor or blender bowl to dislodge any remaining onion and add to the rest of the stock/onion mixture. Bring to a simmer.

4. Add the desired amount of cream. Simmer for 5 minutes.

5. Cream may optionally be used as a garnish. See Leek and Potato Soup (p.83). The best garnish for this soup is fresh chives, finely chopped. Sliced and quickly sautéed green onions are another choice.

Variations

• The soup can be made with a mixture of the onion family building blocks, such as shallots and leeks, instead of, or in addition to the onions.

Ingredients

1 quart chicken, beef, or vegetable stock (p.39)

2 cups basic sautéed onions (p.21) or caramelized onions (p.21)

1 tablespoon garlic purée (p.19)

¼ - 1 cup heavy cream (optional)

salt and pepper to taste

Mushroom Soup

Mushrooms make richly flavored soups. All our mushroom building blocks can be used to make soup. To infuse the beef, chicken, or vegetable stock with a more intense mushroom flavor, we can enlist the help of the dried Porcini mushroom building block.

Mushrooms in Broth Ingredients

1 quart vegetable, chicken, or beef stock (p. 39)

½ - 1 cup Porcini mushroom essence (optional) (p.30)

1-2 cups assorted mushroom building block (p.29), cut into bite-sized pieces

½ cup onion or shallot building block (p. 21)

1 tablespoon garlic purée (p. 19)

salt and pepper to taste

white vermouth or dry white wine (optional)

Mushrooms in Broth

1. Simmer all ingredients together for ½ hour.
2. Serve with fresh-chopped parsley and, for a special treat, a thin stream of white truffle-infused olive oil. This culinary gem is very expensive but very intense, so a teaspoon per serving will be all that is required. Other possible garnishes are fresh tarragon, chervil, chives, or basil. You can also garnish with diced pepper building block (p.25), or concasse tomato (p.11).

   Parmesan bruschette (p.112) complement the soup.

Note: this soup may be used to make mushroom risotto (p.100).

Cream Of Mushroom Soup Ingredients

1 quart beef, chicken, or vegetable stock (p. 39-41).

½ -1 cup Porcini mushroom essence (optional) (p.30)

2 cups duxelle of mushrooms building block (p. 29-30)

1 cup leek building block, puréed (p. 23)

¼ cup garlic purée

salt and pepper to taste

¼ -1 cup heavy cream (optional)

½ cup dry sherry

Cream of Mushroom Soup

For this soup we will be using the duxelle of mushrooms building block (p.29). You may vary the amount of cream or omit it altogether.

1. Place all the ingredients except the cream in a sauce pan.
2. Bring to a boil and simmer 30 minutes.
3. Adjust salt and pepper to taste.
4. Add the cream and simmer for 5 minutes, or use the cream as a garnish, as in the the Leek and Potato Soup (p.83).
5. Serve with Parmesan bruschetta and a fresh herb such as parsley, basil, chives, chervil, or tarragon, or a combination of these herbs.

Herb Roasted Vegetables

The following vegetables may be oven-roasted with dazzling results. Wash all vegetables, and peel them if you desire. It is important that they should also be as dry as possible. Moisture will retard the caramelization of the natural sugars in the vegetables. And that's what makes them taste so damn good!

For each vegetable here are the preparations before roasting.

Peppers

Wash, dry, and cut in half. Remove all seeds—you know who's watching. Slice into ½-inch strips.

Zucchini and summer squashes:

Scrub well and dry. Cut into ½-inch rounds or ½-inch by 2-inch strips.

Winter Squash

(Butternut is the easiest to work with.) Wash, peel, cut in half lengthwise, and scrape out seeds and pulp.
Cut into ¾-inch cubes.

Eggplant

Scrub, dry, and cut into ¾-inch cubes

Onions and shallots

Peel, trimming at root end carefully to leave intact. If the onions are very small, leave whole. Larger onions should be cut into ½-inch wedges. Shallots may be left whole.

Carrots

Choose small, sweet ones – not the big clubs that would choke a horse. Wash, peel, and cut into ¼-inch slices on the diagonal or into round ½-inch coins.

Asparagus

Wash the asparagus to remove any sand.
To find the tender part of the asparagus, bend each spear until it snaps. Discard the root end. If the spears are thick (preferred for roasting), peel with a potato peeler from one inch below the tip to the bottom of the stalk.
Dry on paper towels.

If I have forgotten your favorite vegetable, chill – you can probably oven roast it!

To roast the vegetables:

1. Preheat the oven to 400°

2. Toss each cup of cut vegetables with 2 tablespoons of herb marinade or infused olive oil. The rosemary-thyme oil (p.47) works especially well.

3. Spread the vegetables on the surface of a cookie sheet or roasting pan that has been sprayed with a non-stick spray. This is what God created non-stick pans for.

   Do not overcrowd – we want to give them room to brown. Overcrowding will create steam, which will retard the caramelization.

4. Roast for 30 minutes, turning every 10 minutes. Continue to roast until the vegetables become golden brown around the cut edges. Depending on the oven and vegetables, another 10-20 minutes may be in order.

5. For asparagus roast 5 to ten minutes only.

Polenta

When I was a child, the news that polenta was being served for dinner was enough to send me screaming from the room. Mother dear, usually a fabulous cook, made her polenta very plain, using only water, salt, and cornmeal. Flavorless—to my young taste buds. Mom didn't have a chef in her freezer or know about infusing the water to make polenta something savory and delicious. The addition of herbs to the cooking water makes a world of difference.

If you make herb marinades by the blender method, (p.44) here is a wonderful place to use all that herb residue left behind. The secret to very tasty polenta is to infuse the water with flavor before adding the cornmeal to the water.

It's easy to infuse the water. Simply simmer the residue from making marinade (p.44) or add fresh cut herbs to water and simmer. We are making an herb-infused water that will flavor the polenta. Use ½ cup of marinade residue per quart of water, or ½ cup of thyme, rosemary, bay leaf, and crushed garlic or skins left from roasted garlic. You may want to make the infused water when you make the marinade—simply reduce and freeze. Or you may infuse the water up to one week ahead and refrigerate.

Another possibility is to add some herb marinade or herb-infused oil to the water—one tablespoon per quart.

And if you want to make the polenta extra flavorful, cook it in stock. I recommend chicken or vegetable stock.

As for the polenta itself, there is a choice between fine and coarse cornmeal. There is also "instant" polenta, which cooks quickly, but won't be as creamy as the fine or coarse cornmeals. I don't recommend it. I find that coarse cornmeal produces the best flavor and texture.

I have tried countless recipes for making polenta. Some start with cold water to which polenta is added, then brought to a boil. Some add the polenta to boiling water. I find whisking the cornmeal into boiling liquid works best, when making polenta on the stovetop. Using a whisk as you add the polenta will avoid lumps.

Polenta must be stirred and cooked over a low flame. It has a tendency to "spit" like molten lava if cooked on too high a flame. Be careful—it hurts bare skin! You might consider a heavy rubber glove to protect the hand that stirs.

Thanks to Paula Wolfert's breakthrough cooking method, oven baking, I may never stir another stovetop pot of polenta again.

The consistency of the polenta depends on the ratio of water to cornmeal. For a very soft polenta, use a ratio of 5 or 6 to 1. I prefer a ratio of 5 to 1, which results in a smooth polenta.

Polenta is amazingly versatile. I think Mom would be amazed to see how many possible ways it could be used to tantalize the taste buds. Bland no more!

Basic Polenta

Ingredients

1 cup cornmeal, preferably coarse

5 cups infused water (p. 44) or stock (pp. 39-41) (see above for how to infuse)

1 tablespoon roasted garlic purée

2 tablespoons extra virgin olive oil or infused oil (pp. 45-47) or marinade (p. 44)

1 teaspoon salt and fresh ground pepper to taste

½ cup grated Parmesan cheese (optional, but highly recommended)

Oven baked method

1. Whisk the cornmeal into the water or stock. Add the garlic purée, salt, and pepper. Bring to a simmer, while whisking.

2. Place uncovered into a 350 degree oven. Bake for 45 minutes, stirring every 15 minutes.

3. Stir in Parmesan, taste and adjust salt and pepper

Stovetop method

1. Bring the water or stock to a boil. Add the garlic purée.

2. Quickly pour the cornmeal into the liquid while whisking briskly. Keep whisking until mixture begins to thicken, about 5 minutes.

3. Reduce heat to low flame, and with a wooden spoon, stir the polenta frequently until it is cooked, usually 35-40 minutes. Add more liquid if necessary.

4. Carefully taste and add salt and pepper to taste.

5. Stir in the Parmesan cheese if using.

The polenta is now ready to eat.

Serving Possibilities

Polenta lends itself to many different serving possibilities.

You may spoon the polenta right from the pot or a serving dish. A spoon dipped into hot water makes serving an easier task.

Polenta firms up as it cools, so it can be molded into just about any shape. To make a large polenta cake, I recommend using a springform pan, sprayed with a non-stick spray or brushed with olive oil. Allow the polenta to firm up, then unmold, brush with olive oil, then bake at 400° for about 25 minutes to crisp the outside and heat through.

Or use ramekins or cupcake tins to make individual servings. Just be sure to spray or brush with oil first.

Polenta hors d'oeuvres. Another trick is to employ a madeleine mold, normally used for those little shell-shaped cakes. Mini madeleine molds make perfect hors d'oeuvre-sized bites. Spray the molds with non-stick spray or brush with olive oil, fill each depression with polenta, and allow it to cool until it has firmed up. Invert the mold and lightly tap to remove the polenta "shells." Just before serving, brush them with a bit of olive oil and bake in a 400° oven for 20 minutes to heat through, or longer to form a crisp crust. An instant-read thermometer will tell you quickly when it's hot enough (160°).

You may also microwave them, but there will be no yummy crust formation. Any of the polenta recipes that follow may be served or molded in this way.

Thin polenta cakes. Another idea is to make thin polenta cakes and use them as you would for a "pizza" or "bruschetta" base. See the Pizza and Bruschetta chapter (pp.104-112) for possible toppings. Any of the recipes in that chapter may be used with a polenta-cake base. Use a springform pan or flan rings. Pour in the polenta to form a 1/2-inch-thick disk. If you wish to make several, cool the polenta cake quickly in the freezer, remove and mold the next cake. Add "pizza toppings" and bake as you would for pizza.

Polenta croutons. Another way to use polenta is as a "crouton." Lay a 1/2-inch layer of polenta in a pan, and allow to cool. Remove from pan, cut into cubes, brush lightly with olive oil, and bake until lightly crisp. Add to a soup or salad.

Polenta crisps. You may also use a "cookie cutter" of any shape, and bake the polenta shape in the oven until crisp. Small pieces crisped and impaled on a toothpick make a quick and tasty hors d'oeuvre.

Polenta with Roasted Pepper or Tomato

Add one cup of roasted pepper or tomato to the basic polenta recipe after the cooking is finished.

I recommend rough-chopping the peppers or tomato. The Parmesan is most welcome here. The addition of 1/2 cup onion, shallots, or (especially) leeks will make it that much tastier.

Three Onion Polenta

To the basic recipe, including the Parmesan, add 1/2 cup each of onion, shallot, and leek building blocks. Also, add 1 or 2 tablespoons of fresh chopped chives for color and flavor.

These recipes make basic polenta even more delicious...

Polenta with Gorgonzola Cheese, Walnuts, and Carmelized Onion

Many cheeses besides Parmesan (a must!) complement polenta. A favorite in Italy is to stir in crumbled gorgonzola. Fold quickly or the cheese will melt. I crumble the cheese and then freeze it before adding it to the polenta. This way, bits of cheese remain intact. Toasted walnuts make this version extra delicious. I like to add caramelized onions also. To the basic recipe including the Parmesan cheese, stir in $1/2$ cup of toasted walnuts and $1/2$ cup of caramelized onions.

Polenta with Mozzarella Cheese, Pine Nuts and Basil Purée

Mozzarella cheese, either regular or smoked, is delicious. Cut the cheese into $1/2$-inch cubes and quickly fold into the basic polenta with the Parmesan cheese.

Toasted pine nuts are a wonderful addition. One tablespoon of basil purée may also be stirred into the polenta.

Another way to use mozzarella cheese is to layer it with the polenta. To do this, use a mold. Add enough polenta to cover the bottom of the mold with $1/2$-inch of polenta. Sprinkle with cubes of cheese. Add another $1/2$-inch layer, then more cheese. Repeat until all the cheese and polenta have been used up. Allow to cool, unmold and bake.

Mushroom Polenta

1. Add the mushroom essence to the liquid, if using.

2. Add the roasted garlic.

3. Prepare the polenta as in the Basic Polenta recipe above.

4. When the polenta is cooked, stir in the mushrooms, onion, and Parmesan cheese.

Other Flavorings

There are so many other possible ways to flavor polenta. The following are more ideas. I hope you use them as a guide to create your own custom polenta favorites.

Nuts and seeds. Toasted pine nuts, walnuts, almonds, hazelnuts, or sesame seeds add flavor and texture to the polenta. Stir into the cooked polenta or use as a garnish.

Pitted black olives may be added for color and flavor. Rough-chop them and stir into the polenta when initial cooking is complete.

Mascarpone cheese. For an extra-rich and creamy polenta stir 1 cup of mascarpone cheese into the polenta after it has been cooked. Plan to serve as a side dish—this version will be too soft to mold. A tablespoon of basil purée (p.46) is a wonderful complement.

Tomato or pepper sauces. Any of the tomato or pepper sauces may be used over either a molded or soft-use polenta. Pour a hot ladle of your chosen sauce, just as you would over pasta. The roasted pepper sauce drizzled over the polenta lends a delicious flavor and wonderful eye appeal.

Mushroom Polenta Ingredients

1 cup cornmeal

1 quart infused water, or stock

$\frac{1}{2}$ cup porcini essence (p.30) (optional)

1 tablespoon garlic purée (p.17)

$\frac{1}{2}$ cup onion, shallot, or leek building block (p.20-23)

1 cup mushroom building block (p.29)

$\frac{1}{2}$ cup Parmesan cheese (optional, but highly recommended)

salt and pepper to taste

1 tablespoon fresh, chopped, flat-leaf parsley (optional)

Polenta Surprise

One of my favorite ways to use polenta is to make "Polenta Surprise." "And what is that?" you may ask. Polenta surprise is polenta, layered with some combination of cheese, vegetables, or meat. Layered, cooled, and baked, it makes a very dramatic presentation. Here's one variation:

1. Use oven-roasted, herb-marinated vegetables (p.89) and fresh mozzarella or goat cheese.

2. Use a springform cake pan or a round bowl.

3. Spray well with a non-stick spray or brush with olive oil.

4. To assemble, start with a 1/2-inch layer of freshly made polenta, then scatter the vegetables and cheese over the surface.

5. Cover with more polenta and repeat until you have used up all the vegetable and cheese.

6. You may add any of the toasted nuts.

7. Allow the polenta to cool.

8. Unmold and brush with olive oil. Bake in a 400° oven until a crisp crust is formed and the internal temperature is 160°.

Other Variations

Chicken works well in "Polenta Surprise." I like to use the thighs because the meat is less likely to dry out during the réchauffage (reheating) of the polenta. Cook the chicken as you would for Sauté of Chicken Thigh (p.129). Layer with the polenta as you would for the vegetable and cheese polenta cake. Italian sausage, either sweet or hot, works well here too. In fact, sausage and polenta is a classic combination. Just pan-sauté or roast the sausage until cooked through. Slice into bite-sized pieces. Use like the chicken or the vegetables. Roasted peppers or oven-dried tomatoes can be used to add color and flavor.

Risotto

Risotto is probably the best argument for the value of microwave cooking. Before microwaves, this popular dish required a labor of love—a long time at the stove, patiently stirring and waiting for just the right moment. Microwaves have brought the complex texture and flavor of risotto within the reach of those of us who no longer have the time to stand over the stove the way my grandmother did. Barbara Kafka was responsible for this culinary breakthrough. The traditional method has its merits also. If you are having a dinner party, you can let the guests take turns stirring as you add the hot stock. Make 'em work for their supper! If you have the basic building blocks prepared in advance, risotto becomes even easier.

Risotto requires the correct type of short-grain Italian rice. Perhaps the best known rice for risotto is the plump, medium-grained Arborio. In addition, two other varieties of rice are also useful: Carnaroli, with a firm texture, and Vialone Nano, which cooks more quickly than Arborio, but is less starchy, resulting in a less creamy risotto.

To make risotto, the rice is first sautéed with a little oil and then cooked by adding hot stock, a little at a time. Vegetables, meat or fish are added during the cooking process. All the recipes call for vegetable or chicken stock, although you may use beef stock if you prefer. The two methods for making risotto, the traditional stovetop pour-and-stir, and the much easier microwave pour-and-zap, can be used for all variations on risotto. We will give a master recipe for both methods.

Risotto is a wonderful dish to make for a group. It should be served as soon as it is ready. The Italians like to serve each person a small mound. The eater flattens the outer edge of the mound and eats the flattened part, repeating the process until it's all eaten. This way, the eater eats just the cool edge while keeping the mound warm.

Mushroom risotto

- 2 cups Arborio, Carnaroli, or Vialone Nano rice
- 2 tablespoons infused or plain extra virgin olive oil (p. 45)
- 1/2 cup white wine or vermouth
- 1 cup mushroom building block (p. 29-30), either sautéed or duxelle
- 1/2 cup chopped onion building block (p.21)
- 2 tablespoons roasted garlic building block (p. 19)
- 5 cups chicken or vegetable stock
- 1/2 to 1 cup Porcini mushroom essence (p. 30) (optional). Reduce stock by a similar amount
- 1/2 cup grated Parmesan cheese
- 1 cup boiling water (to be used as needed)
- 1 tablespoon sweet butter
- salt and pepper to taste
- truffle oil
- mascarpone cheese (optional)
- chopped parsley, shredded basil, or toasted pinenuts for garnish (optional)

Risotto the traditional way

A heavy bottomed wide pan is the best for risotto. Enameled cast iron is my personal favorite.

1. In a pot separate from the risotto pan, bring the stock to a boil and then reduce to a simmer. Have the water boiling hot as well. A tea kettle makes this an easy task.

2. Add the rice and olive oil to the pan. (Spray with a non-stick spray for easier cleanup) Over a medium flame, stir the rice and oil together for 2 minutes, stirring to coat and very lightly toast the rice grains. The rice will take on a translucent quality and a small white spot will appear in the center of the grain.

4. Add the wine and stir into the rice. Stir until absorbed, about 2-3 minutes.

5. Stir in the garlic, onions, and mushrooms.

6. Add 1 cup of hot stock and stir constantly until it has been absorbed, about 10 minutes. The rice will begin to soften. Add the Porcini essence.

7. Add more stock in 1/2 cup increments, stirring constantly with each addition. When 4 1/2 cups of stock have been added, begin to taste the rice. Our goal is to have a creamy, cooked rice with an *al dente* bite. If the risotto needs a bit more liquid and you have used up all the stock, use the boiling water to finish, but be careful! If you add too much liquid the rice with burst. It will still be delicious, but it will lack the texture that makes properly made risotto such a sensual delight.

8. When the rice is done, remove from the heat and stir in the butter, then the cheese.

9. Adjust the salt and pepper to taste.

10. For extra delicious risotto fold 1 cup of mascarpone cheese until well blended and drizzle with 2 tablespoons of truffle oil.

11. Garnish with fresh chopped parsley, shredded basil leaves, or, for a real treat, a small handful of lightly toasted pine nuts.

Risotto Microwave method:

Use a microwave-safe dish that is shallow and broad.

1. Spray the dish with non-stick spray for easy cleanup. Toss rice and olive oil together. Leave the dish uncovered throughout the cooking process.

2. In one minute intervals, zap the rice and oil mixture. Stir rice between the intervals. After 3 minutes the rice should be translucent and have the white dot present.

3. Stir in the onions, garlic, and mushrooms.

4. Add 1 cup hot stock and micro-zap on high heat for 10 minutes. Add the Porcini essence.

5. Remove dish from the microwave oven and stir. Add ½ cup hot stock. Stir well. Return to the microwave and zap at high heat for 5 minutes.

6. Continue to stir and add stock as the stock is absorbed into the rice.

7. When the rice is *al dente*, remove and beat in the butter and Parmesan cheese.

8. Garnish with chopped parsley.

Risotto with roasted pepper and mozzarella cheese

1. Depending on process chosen, prepare the rice with the olive oil as in the preceding recipe until the rice is translucent and the white spot is present.

2. Add the white wine, and stir or zap until absorbed.

3. Stir in the peppers, garlic, and onions/leeks.

4. Proceed with the "add stock-stir-absorb" process, as described in the basic recipe, until the risotto is al dente.

5. Stir in the butter and Parmesan cheese, and fold in the mozzarella cheese.

6. Garnish with chopped parsley or shredded basil.

Risotto with pepper and mozzarella Ingredients

2 cups rice

2 tablespoons infused or extra virgin olive oil (pp. 45-46)

½ cup dry white wine or vermouth

1 cup diced roasted red pepper

½ cup onion or leek building block (pp. 20-23)

1 tablespoon roasted garlic purée (p. 17)

5 cups chicken or vegetable stock (pp. 39-40)

1 cup boiling water

4 ounces mozzarella cheese cut into a ¼-inch dice

½ cup grated Parmesan cheese

1 tablespoon sweet butter

chopped parsley or shredded basil for garnish (optional)

Tomato Orange Basil Risotto

Ingredients

2 cups rice

2 tablespoons infused or extra virgin olive oil (pp. 46-47)

grated rind of two oranges. (Use a fine grater and remember to turn the orange frequently, removing only the orange outer skin while avoiding the bitter white pith underneath.)

1/2 cup dry white wine or vermouth

1/2 cup onion, shallot, or leek building block (pp. 21-23)

2 tablespoons roasted garlic purée (p. 19)

juice of two oranges

5 cups chicken or vegetable stock (pp. 39-40)

1 cup boiling water (to be used if needed)

1 cup oven roasted plum tomato (p. 14), or

1 cup well drained concasse tomato (p. 11)

1/2 cup grated Parmesan cheese

2 tablespoons basil purée

1. Stir the rice, oil, and orange rind, and prepare as in previous recipes.
2. Stir in white wine and cook until absorbed.
3. Add the orange juice to rice. Stir until absorbed.
4. Add the onions, garlic, and tomato.
5. Add one cup of stock. Stir or microwave until it is absorbed, then continue adding 1/2 cup until rice is *al dente*.
6. Stir in the Parmesan cheese and the basil purée.
7. Garnish with chopped parsley.

Leek and Shrimp Risotto

1. Heat a sauté pan, add the shrimp—do not overcrowd—and sear. Turn and sear the other side. The shrimp should still be raw in the center. Set aside.

2. Deglaze pan with the white wine and add to the stock.

3. Toss the rice and oil together and sauté or microwave until translucent and white spotted.

4. Stir in the garlic and leeks.

5. Process as for the mushroom risotto.

6. When 4 cups of stock have been added to the rice, fold the shrimp into the rice. Add the next 1/2 cup of stock.

7. Finish the cooking, then beat in the butter.

Garnish with chopped parsley. Do not use the Parmesan cheese garnish.

Leek and Shrimp Risotto Ingredients

2 cups Arborio rice

2 tablespoons infused or plain extra virgin olive oil (pp. 46-47)

5 cups chicken or vegetable stock (pp. 39, 40)

1/2 cup white wine

1 cup boiling water

1 cup leek building block (p. 23)

1 tablespoon garlic purée (p. 19)

2 pounds shrimp, cleaned and de-veined, washed and dried, tossed with 1/4 cup marinade or infused oil

1 tablespoon sweet butter

Pizza and Bruschetta

Who doesn't love pizza, warm and fragrant from the oven? The best pizza is made with your own dough, especially the cornmeal polenta dough whose recipe follows. If that seems like too much work, Italian specialty stores sometimes have pre-made dough in the refrigerator. When very fresh, pre-made dough may be acceptable. Give the dough a good sniff. It should smell slightly yeasty and have a uniform creamy color. Avoid commercial supermarket "pizza doughs" that come in those bang-and-bake tubes.

A delicious alternative to using raw dough is using good quality bread. This is known as bruschetta. Pizza and bruschetta share the same toppings, but the cooking techniques differ. We will first discuss the techniques for making, topping, and baking pizza. Bruschetta recipes will follow.

Pizza

Cornmeal or Polenta dough

1. Sift the cornmeal and flour together. Set aside.

2. Dissolve the sugar or honey in the warm water. An instant-read thermometer will assure the water is the correct temperature.

3. Stir the yeast into the water to dissolve.

4. Allow to stand in a warm place for 5 minutes or until a light beige foam covers the surface.

5. Stir in the oil and salt. If you are using a food processor or electric mixer, skip the next step.

6. If kneading by hand, add the flour, 1/4 cup at a time, stirring until the flour has been absorbed and the dough forms a ball.

Kneading the Dough

By hand

Follow all five preliminary steps above.

1. Lightly flour your work surface and your hands.

2. Using the heel of your hand, push down and away from yourself.

3. Fold the dough in half, turn and repeat.

4. Add a bit more flour, if necessary, to keep the dough from sticking.

5. A dough scraper helps remove bits that stick to the board as you work. A metal spatula works well if you do not own a scraper.

6. Knead until smooth, elastic, springy, and satiny.

7. Once the dough has achieved this state, stop kneading. Over-kneading will result in a tough crust. This process should take approximately 15 minutes.

<u>Pizza Ingredients</u>

1 tablespoon granular sugar or honey

1 1/4 cup warm water (110°F)

1 envelope or 1 teaspoon active dry yeast

2 1/2 cups bread flour

1 cup fine yellow cornmeal

2 teaspoons fine sea salt

1/3 cup infused extra virgin olive oil or plain extra virgin olive oil (pp. 46-47)

1-2 teaspoons very finely chopped fresh (not dried) rosemary or thyme leaves (optional)

Kneading the Dough, continued

Heavy duty food processor.

Follow the preliminary steps for preparing the yeast, through step 5. Use the dough hook attachment if you have one. If not, use the standard blade.

1. Put the flour into the bowl of the food processor. Turn on the machine and pour the yeast mixture through the feed tube.

2. Process until the dough masses around the blade. This should take less than 45 seconds to a minute.

3. Open the cover and feel the dough. If it is still sticky, add a bit more flour, 1 tablespoon at a time, processing between additions.

4. If the dough seems dry, add a bit of water, a teaspoon at a time, until the dough smooths out.

5. Remove dough from the bowl and knead by hand for 2-3 minutes.

Heavy duty mixer.

Follow preliminary steps for preparing the yeast, through step 5.

1. Pour the flour into the bowl of the mixer. Make a well and pour the yeast mixture into it.

2. Using the K blade, gradually raise the speed to medium. Mix until mixture is well blended.

3. Replace the K blade with the dough hook, and knead at medium speed for about 5 minutes.

4. Break off a piece of dough and feel. If it is still sticky add a bit more flour, a tablespoon at a time, until the dough is smooth, satiny and elastic.

5. If the dough seems too dry, add a bit of water, one teaspoon at a time, until dough is smooth, satiny and elastic.

Letting the Dough Rise

Once you have made the dough by one of these three methods, roll it into a ball. Place in a bowl that has been coated with extra virgin olive oil. Turn the dough to coat with oil. Cover bowl tightly with plastic wrap.

For best results let dough rise overnight in the refrigerator. If you are in a hurry, let dough rise for 1 ½ hours in a warm, draft-free 80-85 degree place.

Shaping the Dough

The recipes above will yield four 8-inch pizzas or one 10 x 15-inch rectangular pie.

1. To make round pizza, divide the dough into 4 equal pieces.

2. Shape the pieces into round balls.

3. On a lightly floured surface, flatten the dough with the pads of your fingers and heels of your hands. Work from the center of the dough to the edge, gently prodding and stretching the dough. Leave the dough a little thicker around the perimeter of the pizza.

4. You may also use a rolling pin to flatten the dough. Lightly dust the pin with flour. Always be sure the surface is lightly floured to keep dough from sticking.

Baking the Pizza

There are several methods for baking pizza. The best is to bake it on a hot pizza stone or on tiles. Large pizza stones are available in well-stocked cookware shops. You may assemble your own by buying lead-free, unglazed tiles from a tile dealer. There are two ways to use the tiles: Arrange them on an iron cookie sheet to form a flat baking surface to be placed on the floor of the oven. Or, lay them directly on the floor of the oven. I find the cookie sheet makes them easier to remove. Both methods work if you have a gas oven. If using an electric oven, place the stone/tiles on a rack at the lowest level in the oven. Preheat the oven to 500°F for at least 45 minutes before baking. Yes, we want a red hot oven!

The easiest way to bake pizza is to use a pizza screen. A pizza screen is a flat, round disk of heavy gauge wire mesh with a solid metal border. Pizza screens come in many sizes, from 6 inches to 2 feet. Lightly brush with oil, or spray with a non-stick spray.

1. After shaping the dough as outlined above, lay the dough on the screen.

2. Quickly add the toppings and place on the preheated stone. If you do not have a stone, set the rack on the highest level, and place the screen directly on the rack. A screen is especially useful if you are using a lot of toppings.

3. Add toppings, then bake until the crust is golden brown, about 10 minutes.

To bake directly on the stone—after the dough is formed into a flat disk—lay the dough on a peel. A peel is a flat paddle shaped spatula with a long handle that can range in size from 6 inches to 2 feet. Choose one that will fit comfortably into your oven. If you have ever been to a pizza parlor you may have seen them in action. They come in metal and wood. I find the wooden ones easier to work with.

1. Be sure to lightly dust the peel with flour or fine cornmeal.

2. After you lay the dough on the peel, put the toppings on the pizza, and quickly place in oven (before it sticks).

3. The trick now is to dislodge the pizza from the peel onto the pizza stone/tile. To do this, place the peel over the stone surface and give a few quick jerks. The goal is to leave the pizza dough on the stone/tile to bake.

4. Bake until the crust is golden brown, about 10 minutes.

Pizza may be made in a pan. Heavy gauge, black steel pans are the best. This type of pan absorbs heat well and will not warp in the oven. False bottom tart pans work well too, and make pizza removal easy.

1. Be sure the pan is properly seasoned. Always brush with oil or spray with a non-stick spray.

2. Press the dough into the pan, stretching it to fit to the edge and pushing it slightly up the sides.

3. Add toppings, then bake until the crust is golden brown, about 10 minutes.

Pizza Toppings

When making pizza, it's always best to have all the toppings ready for use. That way you can work quickly once the dough is set to receive them. As soon as the toppings are on the dough, bake the pizza. You don't want the toppings to have time to soak into the dough.

Our pantry has many ingredients that work famously as pizza toppings. Pizzas do not all have tomato sauce and mozzarella cheese. You may use many different vegetable, cheese, meat and fish combinations.

Tomato and cheese

The best tomato sauce to use is the one made from our roasted or oven dried plum tomato sauce. (pp.55-59) These sauces have the least amount of water. Too watery a sauce will result in soggy pizza. Yawn. . . .

If you want to make a pizza without the cheese, I suggest you pre-bake the crust and then add the sauce or building blocks.

Pizza with Tomato Sauce and Mozzarella

In most commercial pizza places the sauce is put on the dough first, then the cheese is added. I like to reverse the process, which allows the cheese to "protect" the dough. The mozzarella from the supermarket that comes vacuum packed in tight plastic results in a rather bland pizza. Seek out handmade mozzarella. It will come packed in salted or unsalted water. Both work equally well. Another possibility is buffalo milk mozzarella. This is usually imported from Italy and has the best texture and a superior flavor. It is also packed in liquid. The flavor and texture of these cheeses, especially the buffalo milk mozzarella, which is very creamy, will be far superior to the mass-market packaged cheese.

The fresh cheeses are a bit more difficult to handle. When you slice them, they tend to weep. To correct the problem, cut the slices of cheese about 1/8-inch thick and lay them on paper towels that have been lightly sprayed with non-stick spray. The towel will absorb the moisture, but the cheese will not stick to the towel. The excess liquid is the sworn enemy of crisp-crusted pizza.

Topping the Pizza

1. Brush the flat surface of the dough with infused or plain extra virgin olive oil.
2. Dust with grated Parmesan cheese (optional but very tasty).
3. Lay the slices of cheese on the dough, leaving ½ inch of cheese-free dough around the edge of the pie.
4. Instead of using the roasted tomatoes puréed as a sauce, you may choose to use them whole or rough chopped.

Other Additions

Roasted garlic building block (p.19). Smear the dough with a bit of roasted garlic purée, or purée the garlic into the olive oil you are using to brush the pizza. I use a ratio of 1 part garlic to 3 parts oil.

Sliced mushroom building block (p.29). One-half cup is about right.

Leek, onion, or shallot building block. Scatter a few tablespoons over the cheese. A pizza covered with buffalo milk mozzarella and caramelized onions (p.21) can be a poem.

Roasted pepper building block (p.24), rough chopped or in strips. Scatter or lay the well-drained pepper pieces over the cheese.

Roasted vegetables. Any from the herb-infused roasted vegetable chapter will work well.

Pitted, oil-cured olives. Crack the olives and remove the pits. Lightly coat with olive oil, and scatter on the surface of the pizza.

Anchovies. Place at the last minute, damp with their oil to keep them from drying out. If you like just a whisper of anchovy flavor, a very light smear of anchovy paste works well. (See Putanesca sauce, p.59.)

Parma ham. Lay thin slices of ham on the surface of the dough after the oil has been brushed. Put the cheese on top. This will prevent it from drying out.

Slices of sausage. If you are using fresh meat sausages, cook them first and then cut into slices ¼-inch thick, and lay on top of the cheese. If using a dry sausage like pepperoni, lay it under the cheese as for Parma ham.

Pepper sauce. For a wonderful change of pace, use the purée of pepper sauce [pp.60] instead of the tomato sauce. Or use a combination of tomato and pepper sauces.

Pesto sauce or basil purée. A thin layer of pesto sauce (p.62) or basil purée (p.46) with either the tomato or pepper sauce will add a complementary flavor. Spread on dough surface before sauce or other toppings.

Goat cheese. I love goat cheese on my pizza. Feel free to add a few slices, or crumble some over the surface. Goat cheese can substitute for mozzarella or complement it.

Garnishes

Two favorites are sesame seeds and pine nuts. These should be scattered on the surface toward the last 2-3 minutes of baking, as they will burn very fast in such a hot oven.

Basil oil drizzled lightly will flavor and add a nice gleam to the pizza. Always add after the pizza has been baked.

If mushrooms are present, a thin drizzle of white truffle oil will add a rich flavor and perfume. Always use after the cooking, as intense heat will destroy the delicate flavor. Heaven!

Rough-chopped, flat-leaf parsley or shredded basil, scattered post-baking, add color and flavor.

Bruschetta

If dough-making seems too much trouble, then bruschetta will be just the thing for you. Bruschetta is a slice of bread with a topping which can be as simple as a rubbing of garlic and a drizzle of olive oil. Or you can use our building blocks to make very tasty combinations quickly and easily. The secret here is to use the best quality bread. Crusty loaves with good texture will make all the difference. And please, please, please! do not use English muffins! The toppings for pizza and bruschettas are interchangeable.

1. Slice the bread about ½-inch thick and lightly toast.
2. Brush lightly with infused or regular extra virgin olive oil. I like to purée roasted garlic and the oil, in a 1-to-4, garlic-to-oil ratio, and use the mixture to brush the slices. These may be served as is, or with any of the pizza toppings and garnishes. Bruschette are especially wonderful with soup or salad.
3. Simply bake in a 400° oven until they are very hot. Like pizza, they are best served immediately.

Parmesan Bruschetta

Sprinkle bread with Parmesan cheese before baking.

Goat Cheese Bruschetta

Spread bread with fresh goat cheese before baking.

Pine nuts or **sesame seeds** add flavor and texture. Sprinkle over bruschetta before baking. Be careful not to over-brown them.

Savory Custard Tarts and Flans

Eggs, milk, half and half, cheese, and building blocks are all you need to create delicious savory tarts or flans (custards). You may be more familiar with these dishes under their generic name— quiches. The savory filling may be baked in a pastry shell or in a flat dish without pastry. One friend suggested "quiche" was passé. "Get a life, Mary," was my first thought, but I sweetly explained that well made savory tarts are ageless, like moi. I don't think well made food is ever out of fashion. The basic recipe for the custard is the same in all the variations, but the combinations of filling change.

As for the pastry crust, I have tried very many over the years and still like Gaston Lenôtre's recipe for pâte brisée the best. A wonderful thing about pastry shells is that they freeze famously and go from freezer to oven. The pastry shell is always pre-baked before being filled with the custard filling and baked. If you are not making your own sweet butter-infused pastry, bake your custard crustless. The pre-made tart shells available in your grocers' frozen food case are a leaden yawn. Why eat all that fat for so little taste and texture reward?

Butter Tart Crust, a.k.a. Pâte Brisée

This recipe for pâte brisée was adapted from Gaston Lenôtre's book, *Faites Votre Pâtisserie comme Le Nôtre*. It has always made the best crust. I have made one change, which is to replace ¼ of the regular flour with cake flour. This reduces the gluten content, resulting in a less elastic dough that is easier to handle. Thanks to Julia Child for this *truc*.

The easiest way to make this dough is to use a mixer with a K or flat blade. You may use a food processor, but be very careful not to overwork the dough. Of course, it may also be made by hand.

Ingredients

1 1/2 cups unbleached flour

1/2 cup cake flour

2 teaspoons granular sugar

1/2 teaspoon salt

7 ounces sweet butter

1 large egg

1 tablespoon milk

1. Sift the flours, salt, and sugar together into the mixing bowl.
2. Cut the butter into small cubes, approximately ½-inch square.
3. Toss the butter into the flour.
4. Add the egg and milk.
5. Mix on medium speed until dough has gathered into a mass around the blade. Be careful not to over-mix.
6. Turn dough onto a lightly floured board and quickly knead into a ball. Flatten into a disk and cover with plastic wrap.
7. Chill for at least 2 hours.

The dough may be frozen at this point and rolled out later, but I prefer to freeze a pre-made tart shell.

1. Lightly dust your work surface (hopefully a plastic pastry board that has been chilled in the freezer) with flour. Remember: anytime you use a pastry or cutting board, a wet paper towel underneath will keep it from sliding.
2. With a rolling pin, gently tap the dough across the surface to flatten it further. Turn the dough 90° and repeat the process.
3. Roll across the dough, flattening it as you roll. Carefully lift the rolling pin after each roll to make sure it isn't sticking. A quick dusting of flour underneath the dough will help. I like to use a powdered sugar shaker filled with flour for this purpose. The goal is to roll out the dough using as little flour as possible.
4. When the dough has been rolled to the desired thickness,

$^1/_{16}$-inch, lightly dust it off with a pastry brush, to remove any excess flour.

5. Roll the dough onto the rolling pin and carefully unroll over the tart pan. I find a false bottom tart pan works best, but any tart or pie pan will work. Carefully lift the dough to fit into the contour of the pan, with as little stretching as possible. Work quickly and with as light a touch as possible for the best results.

6. Roll the pin across the dough and press the dough up the sides so it comes about $^1/_4$-inch above the rim. Using a fork with thin tines, prick the dough all over the surface.

7. At this point wrap with plastic wrap and put into the freezer.

The tart shells may be stored for later use, but even if you plan to use them the same day, I find that freezing them first makes the finishing so much easier.

Most of the recipes will use a partially baked tart shell. This is accomplished when the shell is filled with weights such as beans or special metal pieces known as pie weights.

1. Preheat the oven to 350°

2. Line the tart shell with parchment paper over the dough. To make this easier, crumble the paper into a ball, reopen it, and lay it on the surface of the shell.

3. Add the pie weights.

4. Bake in the oven for 10 minutes.

5. Remove from the oven and carefully lift the parchment and pie weights.

6. Return the shell to the oven for 5 minutes. The goal is to bake the shell until it has just begun to color and swell. This, of course, assumes we are going to fill the shell with a filling and bake it again. It is now ready for one of the fillings discussed later in the chapter.

If the goal is to have a fully baked shell that you are going to fill and not rebake, leave the pie weights in place for 20 minutes. Then, remove them and continue baking until the dough has a light golden brown finish, about 10 to 15 minutes.

<u>Basic Custard Ingredients</u>

3 eggs

1 ½ cups, half-and-half, or whole milk.

½ teaspoon fresh ground pepper

¼ teaspoon salt.

Basic custard filling

1. Ideally all ingredients should be at room temperature. Combine all the ingredients together and beat with a whisk until well blended.

2. Strain the mixture to remove any stray bits of egg shell (quel horreur!). This should produce 2 cups of custard mixture.

The custard batter is now ready to be combined with different building blocks and other ingredients.

The amounts of custard mixture will fill a 9-inch tart shell with the added ingredients. Don't overfill. If there is too much mixture, just bake the excess in a ramekin alongside, a nice perk for the chef!

<u>Infusing Milk Ingredients</u>

1 ½ cups milk or half-and-half

1 carrot, peeled

1 medium onion, peeled

1 stalk celery, well washed

a few Italian parsley stalks

a few roasted garlic skins or a few teeth of garlic

1-2 sprigs of thyme

one bay leaf

Infusing milk

When used in savory recipes, the milk or half-and-half is always much better after it has been infused with aromatic vegetables and herbs. It's really very simple to do for **1½** cups of liquid.

1. Put all ingredients in a food processor and rough chop.

2. Cook with a 2 teaspoons of olive oil for 5 minutes over medium-high heat, stirring as they cook.

3. Stir milk into the mixture, and bring to just below a boil. Cover and let barely simmer for 10 minutes. Steep for at least 1/2 hour or overnight in refrigerator. Strain and use.

If this seems like too much work, relax! The milk or half-and-half will work well uninfused, but infusing it does guild the creamy lily. And remember to infuse anytime you are making a béchamel or soufflé base—it's really so much more delicious.

Roasted Garlic and Fontina d'Acosta Filling

1. Beat the garlic into the custard mixture with a whisk to incorporate it well.
2. Stir in the fontina cheese.
3. Pour into the tart shell or baking dish and bake in a 300° oven until set, about 45 minutes. Baking at 300° gives the custard a very smooth texture.

Roasted Garlic & Fontina d'Acosta Filling Ingredients

2 cups custard mixture (p.116)

1 cup shredded Fontina cheese

$1/4$ cup (or more according to taste) roasted garlic purée (pp.18-19)

Tomato Parmesan Filling

1. Arrange the tomato halves on the bottom of the pre-baked pastry shell or the baking dish.
2. Scatter the olives, if using.
3. Beat garlic into the custard with a whisk.
4. Stir the parmesan cheese into the custard mixture.
5. Pour over the tomatoes and bake in a 300° oven for 45 minutes or until custard is set.

Tomato Parmesan Filling Ingredients

3 cups custard mixture (p.116)

1 tablespoon roasted garlic purée (pp.18-19)

$1/2$ cup grated Parmesan cheese

10-12 oven-dried plum tomato halves (p.14)

1-2 tablespoons pitted black olives, roughly chopped (optional)

Leek and Gorgonzola Filling

1. Stir the leeks into the custard batter, blending well.
2. Gently stir the gorgonzola into the mixture.
3. Pour into a pre-baked tart shell or baking dish, and bake at 300° for 45 minutes, or until set.

Leek and Gorgonzola Filling Ingredients

2 cups custard mixture (p.116)

1 cup leek building block (p.22)

4 ounces gorgonzola cheese, crumbled

Pepper & Smoked Mozzarella Filling Ingredients

2 cups custard

1 tablespoon roasted garlic purée

1 cup rough-chopped roasted pepper building block (p.25), well drained

4 ounces smoked mozzarella cheese, cut into ¼-inch cubes

Pepper and Smoked Mozzarella Filling

1. Beat the garlic into the custard mixture.
2. Stir in the peppers and cheese.
3. Pour into a pre-baked pastry shell or baking dish.
4. Bake in a 300° oven until custard is set for 45 minutes.

Mushroom Shallot/Onion Filling Ingredients

2 cups custard

1 cup mushroom building block, either sliced or duxelle (pp.27-30)

½ cup shallot or onion building block (p.21)

1 tablespoon roasted garlic building block (p.19)

4 ounces goat cheese (optional)

Mushroom Shallot/Onion Filling

1. Beat the garlic into the custard with a whisk.
2. Stir in the mushrooms and shallots/onions.
3. Pour into a pre-baked pie shell or baking dish. Bake at 300° until set.

Note: Goat cheese is a wonderful addition to this tart. Crumble 4 ounces of fresh goat cheese on the bottom of the tart shell or baking dish.

One wonderful tart that does not use a custard filling is a Caramelized onion Tart. If I were asked to choose my last meal, this would probably be the first course!

Caramelized Onion Tart

1. Drain the caramelized onions of any liquid. (This liquid may be added to a soup or sauce)
2. Sprinkle the Parmesan cheese over the bottom of the tart shell.
3. Mix the thyme leaves into the onions. Cover the surface of the tart with the caramelized onions.
4. Bake in a 350° oven for 20 minutes.
5. Sprinkle the surface lightly with very good quality balsamic vinegar.

Ingredients

2 cups caramelized onion building block (p.21)

½ cup grated Parmesan cheese

1 teaspoon fresh thyme leaves (omit if not available)

good quality balsamic vinegar

1 semi-baked tart shell.

Possible additions to the tart:

Goat Cheese. Fresh or aged goat cheese, scattered over the surface before baking, will add a creamy counterpoint to the sweet onions. Four ounces is about right.

Mozzarella cheese, especially creamy buffalo milk mozzarella, is a delicious addition. Place on the surface of the tart before baking

Black olives. Use good quality, definitely not the bland canned variety. Be sure to remove the pits. (See putanesca sauce, p.59, for more information about pitting them.) Scatter the olives over the surface before baking.

Anchovies. Use good quality, packed in olive oil. Lay them on the surface before baking. (See putanesca sauce, p.59.)

Pine nuts. Pine nuts toast quickly, so they should be scattered on the surface 2-3 minutes before the tart is finished baking. Or lightly toast them first and put on the bottom of the tart before you cover with the onions.

Shellfish and Fish Dishes

Shellfish and fin fish have the virtue of quick cooking. Combine quick cooking with the speed of our primary building blocks, and you have delightful results in short order.

Sautéed shrimp and scallops

Shrimp are the most versatile shellfish. Their flavor marries well with every one of our basic building blocks. They cook quickly and are delicious. Talk about fast food!

The easiest way to cook shrimp is in a sauté pan. The goal is to sear the shrimp quickly and finish them with the building blocks.

Shrimp with Garlic Sauce

1. Mix the shrimp and the marinade or oil together with the fresh ground pepper. If possible, allow the shrimp to marinate for a couple of hours, although you may sauté immediately.

2. Heat a sauté pan over high heat for 1 minute. Away from flame, spray the pan with non-stick spray (highly recommended, but not essential).

3. Add the shrimp, but do not crowd them. If too many are put into the pan at once, they will not brown properly. Cook in batches if necessary. Sear one side; turn over; and sear the other side. (Sear about 2 minutes per side. The shrimp should still be a bit raw in the middle when they are removed from the pan.) Place in a dish or bowl and cover lightly with foil.

4. Adjust the heat and continue to cook the rest of the shrimp until all are seared. Be careful not to burn the residue in the pan.

5. After searing the last batch of shrimp, remove. Add the wine or stock to the pan and scrape up any cooked-on bits. (They will add extra flavor to the sauce.)

6. Add the garlic and lemon juice, reduce the liquid by ⅔.

Ingredients

- **1 pound shrimp (16-20 count), peeled and deveined, quickly rinsed and patted dry with paper towels**

- **¼ cup rosemary, thyme, bay leaf and garlic marinade (pp.44-45) or infused olive oil (pp.46-47)**

- **½ teaspoon fresh ground pepper**

- **½ cup dry white wine, vermouth, or dry sherry**

- **½ cup vegetable or chicken stock (pp.39-40) (or omit and use 1 cup wine)**

- **2 tablespoons fresh squeezed lemon juice (better to omit this than use that battery acid in green bottles or plastic lemon containers)**

- **2-3 tablespoons roasted garlic purée (p.19)**

- **1-2 tablespoons fresh chopped Italian parsley**

7. Add the shrimp and mix them well into the sauce.

8. Cook until the shrimp are just cooked through. They should be opaque in the center. If you cook shrimp a lot, you will develop a sense of when they are done. In the meantime when you think they are ready, cut off a piece, blow, and take a bite.

9. Garnish with the parsley and lemon wedges.

Variations

Every variation here works well with the garlic sauce. You may omit the garlic or reduce the amount according to your taste, but I say, "Go for it!"

Add ½ cup of one or more of the following to the liquid in step 5 above:

• sautéed or (roasted) **onions/shallots** (p.21)

• **leeks** (p.23)

• oven-roasted or **concassé tomatoes** (p.11-12)

• sliced **mushrooms** (p.29)

• **rough-chopped peppers** (The addition of sherry will give this dish a Spanish flavor, especially in combination with the peppers—muy bueno!) (p.25)

• One or two teaspoons of good **balsamic vinegar** may be added to the wine/stock in step 4. This is especially delicious with the tomato addition.

• **Sea scallops** may be used instead of shrimp. Seek out nice, plump specimens with a lustrous sheen. To prepare for the sauté, pull off the muscle on the side of the scallop. Quickly rinse in water and pat dry on paper towels. Toss in the marinade and, as with the shrimp, cook quickly to sear the outside. Scallops will release a lot of liquid if not quickly seared. Finish as for the shrimp, being careful not to overcook the scallops. They should be just opaque in the center.

Fish Filets

Many types of fish also lend themselves to the quick sauté method. There is one difference in the preparation steps. After the fish is cooked, it is not returned to the pan with the sauce. Unlike shrimp or scallops, the cooked fish is fragile. So the sauce is made separately and served with the fish. Exceptions to this rule are monkfish, tuna, and swordfish, which are firm enough to be returned to the pan with the sauce without breaking up.

Among the most useful fish for sautéing are snapper, cod, sea bass and striped bass, monkfish, tuna, and swordfish.

Ideally, use bone-free filets or steaks. To serve with or without skin is a matter of taste. If you want to cook the fish with the skin, make sure all scales have been removed. Scales in your mouth are groady to the max.

Fish Filet Sauté

1. Heat a sauté pan over high heat for one minute.

2. Add the oil.

3. Dust one filet at a time in seasoned flour. Place the filet in the hot oil, skin side down. Sauté until crisp. Turn; cook until the other side is crisp. Do not overcook—the flesh should be just translucent. To check, use an instant-read thermometer (120°F is about right). If you don't have a thermometer, use a small, sharp knife to make a small slit in the filet and examine the flesh. Forget that "cook until flakey" advice. Flakey = dry!

4. Remove the filet with a flat spatula to a platter. (Cover with foil and place in a warm spot.) Repeat for each filet.

5. Add the wine or stock to the pan and scrape up any cooked-on bits. They will add extra flavor to the sauce. (Any of the flavor-enhancing building blocks used for the shrimp sauté work well here also—onions/shallots, leeks, oven-roasted or concassé tomatoes, sliced mushrooms, chopped peppers.)

6. To serve, pour sauce on plate. Lay fish filet skin side up on top of the sauce. Garnish with chopped Italian parsley and lemon wedges.

Fish Filet Sauté ingredients

1 pound fish filets, skinless and boneless is my first choice

¼ cup seasoned flour (¼ cup of unbleached white flour with 1 teaspoon each of fine sea salt and fresh ground pepper blended into it)

⅛ cup herb-infused or regular extra virgin olive oil (p.46)

½ cup dry white wine, vermouth, or dry sherry

½ cup vegetable or chicken stock (pp.39-40) (or omit and use all wine)

2 tablespoons fresh squeezed lemon juice (better to omit this than use that battery acid in green bottles or plastic lemon containers)

¼ cup roasted garlic purée, (p.19)

1 tablespoon chopped Italian parsley

Salmon

Salmon is a delicate fish that really needs very little to make it delicious. Salmon is a fish for which garlic is a bit too strong. However a rosemary/thyme marinade will complement the salmon well. I find rosemary is the perfect herb for salmon. If you are lucky enough to have access to lemon thyme, use it also. Remember, never use a marinade with an acid ingredient, e.g., lemon juice or vinegar, with fish, as this will cause the flesh to become mushy. Add the acid to the finishing sauce. Salmon is full of fat so there will be a lot of fat left after you sauté it.

My favorite way to finish salmon is with balsamic vinegar and lemon juice. And if you have them on hand, caramelized onions, shallots, or leeks will make this a dish fit for a king.

Ingredients

1 pound salmon filet or steak.

$\frac{1}{8}$ cup rosemary/thyme marinade, made without acid (p.45)

2 tablespoons balsamic vinegar

1 tablespoon fresh squeezed lemon juice

1 cup caramelized onions or shallots. (The leek building block also works very well here.) (pp.21, 23)

Salmon with Rosemary/Thyme Marinade, finished with Balsamic Vinegar and Caramelized Onions

I prefer to use boneless salmon filet, as I hate finding bones in my mouth while eating fish. An eyebrow tweezer makes a nifty tool for removing any bones embedded in the flesh. Just grab the tip of the bone and yank.

1. Rub marinade over the salmon. If possible, allow to infuse for an hour or more in the refrigerator.

2. Heat a sauté pan for one minute over high heat. Spray with non-stick spray.

3. Add fish, skin-side-down. Reduce heat to medium high; cook for 2 minutes; turn and cook 2 minutes more. This should leave the flesh just cooked through in the center.

4. Remove from pan and place on a warm plate. Loosely cover with foil. Pour off the excess fat.

5. Add the balsamic vinegar and lemon juice to the pan. Scrape up any cooked on bits and reduce by 2/3.

6. Add the caramelized onion, shallots, or leeks to the pan and heat through.

7. Place the onion, shallots, or leeks on a plate and lay the cooked filet over it. Drizzle with any juice the fish has released while resting.

8. Garnish with chopped flat-leaf parsley, basil, or chives.

There are other ways to garnish the salmon filet besides the caramelized onions, shallots, or leeks. Both roasted peppers and roasted tomatoes make a fine garnish. Just add ½ cup of either to the balsamic/lemon reduction and heat through.

Grilled Fish

Sautéing fish has the advantage that it's easy to make a great sauce afterwards. But since people are mad for grilling, let's discuss how our building blocks apply to great grilling. Our marinades sans acid will add flavor and help keep the fish moist during the cooking. For each pound of fish use 1 tablespoon of marinade. The rosemary-thyme-bay leaf-garlic (p.47) works very well with most fish except salmon. Omit the garlic for the salmon.

The secret to great broiled or grilled fish is to expose the fish to high heat. This will quickly sear and seal the flesh and keep the inner flesh moist. Always pre-heat broiler or grill for at least 10 minutes before starting cooking. If using charcoals, wait until they are white hot.

Ingredients

1 pound fish filet, cut to an even thickness for even cooking. I recommend 1-inch.

2 tablespoons of herb marinade (pp.44-45)

salt and pepper

lemon for garnish

Grilled Fish Filets

1. Brush marinade over both sides of fish. Allow to sit for 1 hour, if possible.

2. Preheat grill or broiler

3. Sear fish under or over grill. Cook 5 minutes. Turn and cook 5 minutes more. The trend has been to cook the fish "rare," a.k.a. "raw," in the center. Of course it's a matter of taste, but do not overcook or the fish will be dry. Use an instant-read thermometer. Around 100° will be rare. Remember the fish will continue to cook once removed from the heat—the temperature will rise by at least 5°. If you prefer, cook fish until it is 120°. It should be just opaque.

4. To finish the fish, one of the following will add extra flavor and pizzazz:

   Infused oil (p.45)—drizzle a bit of flavored olive oil over fish.

   For each pound of fish a drizzle of **balsamic vinegar**—about 1-2 teaspoons per pound of fish.

   Lemon juice—always use fresh-cut lemons. Anything else has no place in a serious kitchen.

   One of the **tomato** or **pepper sauces** may be served (pp.55-61). Use as a garnish over fish, or as a bed underneath.

Chicken

Chicken is a delicious blank canvas on which to paint a flavorful picture. Whenever possible use free-range chickens, as they are usually the tastiest. While I was living in Paris, I was hired to cook in Normandy for a holiday week. I was lucky enough to buy chickens directly from a farmer who raised free-range chickens, which he also fed cracked corn mixed with *herbs de provence*. Never have I eaten such delicious chicken—absolute heaven. Proust had his madeleines; I will always have my Normandy chicken.

Buying. But back to reality – if buying whole chickens, you may want to remove the breast and thighs yourself and save the rest of the bird for the stock pot. Otherwise, breasts and thighs are available both with skin and skinless, with bones and boneless. All variations work well in the following recipes. Chicken cooked with the bone will be more flavorful. Boneless is more convenient for eating. Skinless breast and thigh will be lower in fat. If calories are a concern, cook the chicken with skin on and then remove it after cooking. The fat in the skin adds flavor and helps keep the meat moist.

Preparation. Always rinse and dry the chicken. The blood in the cavity will be the first thing to spoil, so it's best to rinse it away. Pat dry with paper towels, and be careful where you drip the rinse water. Remember that chicken is a source of salmonella and other food-borne microbes that can result in food poisoning. Great care should be taken to wash hands, knife, and board well to avoid contamination of other foods. A light bleach and water solution will accomplish this.

When preparing chicken, meat, or fish, I usually line the work surface under the cutting board with plastic wrap. This makes for a very easy cleanup. One last hint: a wet paper towel laid under the cutting board will keep it from slipping.

Cooking. In most of the recipes that follow, the chicken will be cooked in a sauté pan or oven-roasted to take advantage of the pan residue, which combines well with the building blocks to make a bit of sauce. Please keep in mind that herb-marinated chicken will grill or broil beautifully. If you desire a sauce, you might consider one of the tomato, roasted pepper, or garlic sauces (p.54).

To insure quick and even cooking, pound the breast and thigh to an even thickness. This is very simple to accomplish: lay the breast or thigh down flat on a cutting board, skin side up. Cover with a piece of plastic wrap, a plastic bag, or heavy duty foil. Strike with the flat side of a chef's knife or cleaver until the breast is flattened to an even thickness. The chicken part is now ready to use.

Thighs are usually sold on the bone. To remove the bone, not necessary but sometimes desired, lay the thigh, skin side down, on the cutting board. Feel for the bone and make a cut the length of it. Pull out and cut meat free on either end.

Marinades. Chicken will benefit from a turn in one of the marinades or infused oils (p.44-47). The rosemary, thyme, bay leaf and garlic marinade is my favorite (p.44). Chicken should marinate for a few hours, or—better yet—for an overnight stay. But even a quick dip will add to the flavor. Rub the breast or thigh with the marinade. If using chicken with skin attached, be sure to rub the marinade under the skin of the chicken. The flavor will permeate the meat better this way.

Sauté of Chicken Breast or Thigh

1. Heat a frying pan over high flame for 30 seconds. Remove from heat.

2. Step away, and then spray the frying pan with a thin film of non-stick spray.

3. Add the breast or thighs, skin side down, and reduce the temperature to medium high. For quick cooking, place a weight on the chicken. To do this, cover the breast with a piece of foil sprayed with a non-stick spray, or parchment paper. This is not necessary, but it will help reduce the splatter of sizzling fats as the chicken cooks. Place a pot filled with hot tap water on the foil or parchment paper. The result is a very crisp skin—the best part of this dish. This very popular Italian method of cooking is known as *Pollo al Mottone* or chicken cooked under a brick. If you omit the weight and sauté uncovered, invest in a splatter screen—it makes stove cleanup much easier.

4. Cook for 5 minutes, until skin is very crisp and golden brown. Uncover and turn, cooking the other side until browned. The breast should be cooked through, to 165°. Check with instant-read thermometer, or cut a slit and examine the juices. The juices should run clear. Chicken thighs will usually need an extra 1-2 minutes more per side in the sauté pan. Be careful not to burn the pan's cooked-on juices.

5. Remove the chicken from the pan and pour off any accumulated fat. Remove the skin now, if desired, and set chicken aside in a warm place.

6. Immediately add the stock/wine/water and return to high heat.

7. Deglaze by scraping the cooked-on residue into the liquid, and reduce the liquid by $1/2$ or more, depending on how concentrated you want the sauce to be.

8. Add salt and pepper to taste.

9. If you want to add a French accent at this point, whisk a teaspoon or 2 of sweet butter into the sauce.

Ingredients

1 8-ounce chicken breast or 2 thighs, flattened and marinated in one of the herb marinades (pp.44-45)

1 tablespoon marinade or infused oil per breast or set of thighs

$1/2$ cup chicken stock, white wine, water, or a combination of these. Chicken stock and white wine will produce the most flavorful sauce.

Salt and pepper to taste.

For a Spanish accent use half dry sherry and half chicken stock. Olé!

Serving. There are several ways to serve the chicken. If the chicken is being served skinless, pour the sauce over the chicken. If the chicken has a crisp skin, pour the sauce on the plate, and set the chicken, skin side up, in the sauce.

We can easily use our building blocks to enhance the chicken and sauce. In the recipes below, the amount of building block is given as a rough guide—add more or less according to your taste. All amounts are given for one breast or two thighs, so just multiply by the number you are cooking to determine the amounts to use.

Chicken with Garlic

Add one half to one whole tablespoon roasted garlic building block to the deglazing liquid (p.19). Cook until sauce is reduced. This makes a garlic-rich sauce.

You may add a bit of cream or crème fraîche, say 1-2 tablespoons, if calories are not a problem. This will make a very rich, creamy sauce.

Chicken with Leeks

Adding ¼ to ½ cup of leek building block to the liquid will contribute the leeks' creamy texture and flavor to the sauce. (p.23)

Chicken with Caramelized Onion

Add ¼ to ½ cup of caramelized onions to the liquid (p.21). A teaspoon of balsamic vinegar will enhance the natural sweetness of the onions.

Chicken with Roasted Pepper

Add ¼ to ½ cup of chopped pepper or pepper purée to the liquid (p.25). Any pepper nectar maybe used as part of the deglazing liquid (p.25). A tablespoon of dry sherry is a nice addition to the deglazing liquid. A tablespoon of roasted garlic purée and a few tablespoons of onion, leek, or shallot building block will make this even better.

Chicken with mushrooms

Add ¼ to ½ cup of one of the mushroom building blocks (p.27) to the liquid. Here is the perfect time to use porcini mushroom essence (p.30) in the liquid portion. Use ⅓ essence to ⅔ stock/wine/water. The addition of garlic and onion building block will enhance the flavors as well. A few tablespoons of rough chopped pepper (p.24) will add flavor and visual appeal.

Chicken with tomato

Any of the tomato building blocks will work well here (p.10). Add ¼ - ½ cup to the liquid, with a little oregano. In addition, a tablespoon of garlic, and onion, leek, or shallot building blocks will add sweetness and flavor. Mushroom and pepper may also be added to make a more complex sauce. For some heat add a scant half tablespoon of cayenne pepper. For a bit of extra soleil grate some orange or lemon rind into the deglazing liquid. A bit of juice would be good also, say, a tablespoon of lemon or ½ cup of orange. Only fresh-squeezed need apply. This is a quick way to make delicious "chicken cacciatore." Mama mia!

Whole Chicken (French Roasted Chicken, Cornish Hen, or Poussin)

When I'm asked as a chef, "What is your favorite dish?" I always answer, "perfectly roasted chicken." One of the best things I learned at the Cordon Bleu cooking school is how to French-roast a chicken. I have been refining and experimenting with the technique ever since. With chicken stock and marinade building blocks on hand, the recipe is very simple to prepare. The secret to this dish is to roast the bird, breast side down, in aromatic liquid for part of the roasting process. Roasting in a bath of rich chicken stock and white wine yields delicious, moist meat, and the liquid becomes the basis for a great sauce. But first, the chicken needs a coating of marinade. Any of the thyme/rosemary combinations work well. This recipe works for all sizes of chickens from capons to poussins, and for turkey, pheasant or quail.

1. Loosen the skin over the breast and on the sides of the thighs, but be careful not to tear.
2. Place chicken in a bowl and pour the marinade so it runs under the skin. With your fingers rub to cover the flesh.
3. Rub the inside cavity of the chicken with the marinade.

Ingredients

Chicken—I prefer a 2-3 pound chicken, a 1 pound poussin, or a 1 pound cornish hen

Enough marinade to cover the bird, about ¼ cup (pp.44-45)

Chicken stock (p.40) and white wine, approximately 1 cup, enough to cover the bottom of baking dish to a depth of 1 inch

131

4. If time allows, let the bird marinate in the refrigerator for a few hours or overnight.

5. Preheat oven to 500°.

6. Place chicken in a shallow baking dish, breast side up. Ideally, the baking dish should be just large enough to hold the bird with an inch of space around it.

7. Put the bird in the oven and reduce heat to 400°.

8. Roast for 10 minutes; this will tighten the skin.

9. Remove from the oven, turn the chicken breast-side-down, and add liquid.

10. Baste the bird and return to the oven. A bulb baster works very well here. If you don't have one, use a spoon. Baste every 15 minutes, skimming the liquid from the surface, which will be the most fatty. Roast until the skin is golden brown and the internal temperature of the chicken is 150°. This should take about 45 minutes.

11. Remove chicken from pan and pour off the juices.

12. Skim off the fat and save the remaining liquid for the sauce.

13. Return the chicken, breast-side-up, to the roasting pan. Pour the skimmed fat from step 12 into the pan.

14. Baste the chicken with the skimmed fat and return to oven. Repeat every 5 minutes, baking until the thigh meat registers 165°.

15. When done, remove from oven and let rest for 5 minutes in a warm place. This rest will allow the chicken's juices to return back into the flesh. If you cut the chicken too soon it will "bleed" its juices.

16. During the chicken's final roast and rest, reduce the stock by 75%. If the stock still has a little fat, gently drag a paper towel across the surface to absorb the remaining fat. Carve the chicken and serve with the sauce. If desired, any of the building block additions used earlier in the chicken chapter may be used in this sauce. Just stir them in and simmer 5 minutes or more.

Poached Chicken

Chicken cooked slowly in a good chicken stock results in a delicate and delicious bird. With chicken stock from our pantry, poached chicken is quick and easy to prepare. A whole chicken or pieces work equally well. The stock will be extra-rich after the cooking. The chicken adds more flavor to the already flavorful stock.

1. Wash and drain the chicken.

2. Place in a pot and add stock to cover.

3. On high heat, bring to a boil, then reduce to a simmer.

4. Skim off foam and fat as the chicken cooks. A whole chicken will take approximately 1 hour; cut-up parts will take about half that. Use an instant-read thermometer to test for the correct temperature.

5. Cook until chicken reaches an internal temperature of 165°.

6. Remove, wrap with foil, and set in a warm place.

7. Skim the fat from the chicken stock.

8. Serve the chicken in pieces in the warm stock, or reduce the stock by ⅔ and use as a sauce. You may add leek building block (p.23) for extra flavor.

Ingredients

Whole chicken or chicken parts

Chicken stock to cover (p.40)

Stuffed Rolled Breast

Chicken breasts, boned and pounded flat, are easy to stuff with delicious fillings made from the building blocks. The trick is to spread the chosen filling on the breast and then roll the breast into a cylinder.

1. Remove skin, set aside.

2. To prepare the breast, place on a cutting board and lay a piece of plastic, a plastic bag (the zip close kind) or heavy duty foil over the breast. Pound with the flat part of a meat pounder (best), chef's knife, or a cleaver. Strike the meat across its length side to side to form a flat piece of even thickness.

3. Spread the chosen filling over the surface of the chicken (see below for fillings), and roll up into a cylinder.

4. Drape the skin from step 1 over the chicken cylinder. The skin will keep the meat moist during the cooking process. You can easily remove the skin before serving, or eat it— as your waist and arteries dictate.

Toothpicks or a bit of string will help the rolled chicken pieces hold their shape while they cook. If using toothpicks, use three: pierce the roll at each end and in the middle. If using string, tie a loop around each end and one in the middle.

There are three methods of cooking the roulades. You may poach them as outlined in the preceding recipe. Cook until the internal temperature is 165°. Pan sautéing or oven-roasting (recipes follow) both work well also.

Pan Sauté Roulade

1. Heat a sauté pan over medium-high heat for one minute. Away from flame, spray with a non-stick spray. Add 1 tablespoon of infused or plain extra virgin olive oil or marinade (pp.44-45).

2. Add the rolls, seam side down, and cook on all sides over medium-high heat until evenly browned. The internal temperature should be 165°.

3. Remove from pan and cover with foil. Keep in a warm place.

4. The pan may be deglazed, as discussed in the chicken sauté recipe (p.129).

Oven-Roasted Roulade

1. Place the roulades in a shallow roasting pan, seam side down. Choose a pan large enough to hold them with about an inch between the rolls.

2. Bake in a 500° oven until they reach an internal temperature of 165°.

3. Remove from the roasting pan and cover with foil to keep warm.

4. Deglaze the pan as discussed in the chicken sauté recipe (p.129).

Roulade Fillings:

Garlic. Purée of roasted garlic is a natural for this technique (p.19). Spread $1/2$ - 1 tablespoon over the surface of the breast. You may want to scatter some fresh thyme leaf or chopped Italian parsley over the surface. Lightly toasted sesame seeds or finely chopped nuts add flavor and texture. Sprinkle with a bit of sea salt and fresh ground pepper.

Mushrooms. Duxelles (p.29-30) are a natural for stuffing chicken. Just spread a layer over the surface. Sliced sautéed mushrooms may be finely chopped and used in the same way. A food processor is indispensable for this task. Two to three tablespoons per breast is about right. You may want to spread a bit of roasted garlic first and add the mushrooms to the garlic and herbs. You may add nuts here also. Sprinkle with a bit of sea salt and fresh ground pepper.

Caramelized onions or shallots. Spread a layer of the onions or shallots (p.21) over the surface of the chicken breast, 2-3 tablespoons per breast. A scattering of fresh thyme or chopped Italian parsley adds extra flavor. A dusting of Parmesan cheese complements the onion/shallot layer. Sprinkle with a bit of sea salt and fresh ground pepper.

Leeks. Leek building block (p.23) is perfect for filling chicken, as leeks and chickens go so well together. Just spread $1/2$ cup over the breast. Sprinkle with a bit of sea salt and fresh ground pepper.

Tomato. Use the oven roasted tomato building block (p.14) and make a thick purée with a bit of infused olive oil and roasted garlic (p.19). Half a cup of tomato, $1/2$ tablespoon of garlic, and $1/2$ tablespoon of infused or plain extra virgin olive oil puréed in a food processor or blender will make a delicious paste to spread over the breast.

Peppers. Roasted peppers (p.25) make a delicious filling for chicken. They may be used either whole or puréed. For whole peppers, spread a bit of roasted garlic on the surface of the breast. Lay strips of drained, roasted pepper over that.

Pepper purée (pp.25-26) needs to be thickened a bit to be used as a filling. This is easy: purée the pepper. You may want to add some roasted garlic or leek. A ratio of 3 parts pepper to 1 part garlic or leek is about right. Cook in a sauté pan over a medium heat until the purée thickens, about 10 minutes. Allow the purée to cool to room temperature. If time is urgent, place the pan over cold water with ice cubes.

Spread the purée over the surface of the breast. Chopped, lightly toasted pine nuts and chopped Italian parsley are tasty additions. Sprinkle with sea salt and fresh ground pepper to taste.

Goat cheese. Any of the above fillings may be combined with fresh goat cheese to make a delicious filling. Use equal parts goat cheese to building blocks except for garlic. With garlic use a ratio of four parts goat cheese to one part garlic, unless you have a date with a vampire.

Parma Ham. A slice of Parma ham is another possible addition.

Ingredients

1 pound of chicken breast, trimmed of all bone, skinned, and cut into 1-inch pieces. A bit of fat is OK unless calories are a concern.

2 large eggs

¼ cup onion, shallot, or leek building block (pp.21, 23)

¼ cup flat leaf parsley, loosely packed

1 tablespoon roasted garlic (p.19)

1 tablespoon infused or plain olive oil (p.46-47)

1 teaspoon fresh thyme leaf or 2 teaspoons herb marinade (p.44-45)

½ teaspoon sea salt

½ teaspoon fresh ground pepper

2 tablespoons dry sherry or white vermouth (optional)

Chicken Mousse

Now here is a dish that will impress your guests and is a snap to make. The mousse is a combination of chicken breast, eggs, and building blocks, puréed together and baked. It's great hot or cold and lends itself to endless variations.

1. Place everything into the bowl of a food processor.
2. Purée until mixture is very smooth.
3. Fry a teaspoon of mousse and taste. Adjust salt and pepper if necessary.
4. Scrape into a well greased pan lined with a piece of parchment paper. Almost any oven-proof pan will work. Just be sure to grease well. One trick I like to use is to put the baking dish in the freezer. Then brush the inside with infused or plain olive oil or melted butter. Large or individual soufflé dishes work well. Non-stick muffin pans work very well to make a lot of individual mousses. Loaf pans, especially non-stick ones, are also good choices.
5. Bake in a 350° oven until an instant-read thermometer inserted into the center reads 165°. The cooking time will depend on the thickness of the mousse and the choice of pan. But start to check after 30 minutes.
6. When done, allow to cool for 10 minutes, loosely covered with foil.
7. Unmold and serve plain or with one of the suggested sauces listed at the end of the recipe.
8. Any juices left should be added to the sauce or drizzled over the mousse.

Variations

Mushroom. Add 1 cup of duxelles or sliced mushrooms (p.29) to the mousse after the initial purée step. You may either purée them into the mixture or fold the mushrooms into the mousse with a rubber spatula. Folding will keep the mushroom pieces intact. This way you can control the size of the mushroom pieces in the mousse. A tablespoon of porcini mushroom essence (p.30) will deepen the mushroom flavor.

Tomato. After the purée step fold 1/2 cup of rough-chopped oven roasted tomato (p.14) into the mousse.

Leeks. Leeks and chicken are a splendid taste combination. Fold 1/2 cup of leeks (p.23) into the mousse or gently pulse in, using the food processor blade, until the leeks are just mixed into the mousse. Be careful not to over-mix.

Peppers. Use ½ cup of well drained, rough-chopped peppers (p.25). Add to the mousse in the same way as for the leeks.

Caramelized Onion/Shallot. Add ½ cup, using the same method as for the leeks.

Nuts. Lightly toasted nuts: almonds, walnuts, pecans, pine nuts, or pistachios add wonderful texture and flavor. Add about ½ cup after the purée step. Pulse or fold into the mousse the same way as for the leeks.

Herbs. Tarragon or chervil may be added with the parsley.

Sauces for chicken mousse

Many of the tomato and pepper sauces from earlier chapters (pp.55-60) may be used with the mousse. Another possible embellishment is to drizzle basil oil (p.46) over the cooked chicken mousse. A quick sauce may be made by reducing chicken stock, onion, and garlic:

Chicken demi-glace sauce with onions and garlic

1. In a saucepan combine all the ingredients and bring to a boil.
2. Lower the heat to a strong simmer and reduce the liquid by ⅔.
3. Adjust salt and pepper to taste.
4. The sauce may be used as is or puréed. If you are puréeing in a blender, read instructions on page 14.

Ingredients

2 cups chicken stock (p.40) and any juice from the mousse

½ cup onion building block (p.21)

1 tablespoon garlic (p.19)

1-2 tablespoons dry sherry, white wine, or vermouth

Veal, Beef, Lamb, and Pork

You can cook veal, beef, lamb, or pork to great advantage using our building blocks. Use tender cuts that lend themselves to a hot sauté pan or broiler for quick cooking and succulent eating. These are always the most expensive cuts. But better a smaller portion of tender succulent meat than a slab of tough flesh a wolf would have trouble chewing.

One of my favorite cuts of meat is a beautiful veal, pork, or lamb chop. The best are cut from the loin or rib. When cut an-inch thick, they will cook quickly but stay moist inside. I prefer to leave the meat on the bone, as it will have more flavor. However, a filet of any of these cuts will work very well also. When it comes to beef, tender steaks are where it's at. Filet of beef is very popular but somewhat lacking in flavor. My favorite steak is a well-marbled shell steak. A one-inch cut is perfect, although filet may be cut thicker with good results.

To really enhance the meat's flavor, marinate it in one of the marinades on page 43. The best flavor is achieved if the meat rests at least 12 hours in the marinade. Twenty-four hours is ideal. A quick rest is better than no rest and will add considerable flavor. Always trim off any excess fat first. Lightly coat the meat in marinade. Place in a shallow dish or plastic bag and let it rest in the refrigerator.

The meat can be grilled or sautéed. I prefer the sauté method because the pan can then be deglazed to make a quick, delicious sauce. Deglazing is one of a chef's best trucs. Liquid is added to the pan after the meat has been cooked and excess fat poured off. Water, wine, or stock, or a combination of these, combine with the pan residue to make a quick, flavorful sauce.

Sautéed Veal, Pork, Lamb Chops, and Beef Steak

The amount of cooking time will depend on the thickness of the chop or steak. The goal is to cook it until the center is pink and the outside well caramelized, except for pork, which needs more cooking. For veal, lamb, or beef, cook until the internal temperature is 120° for rare. Pork should be cooked until it reaches 150°. Don't overcook it, or it will be dry and tough. I find an instant-read thermometer indispensable! The best way to test is to grab the meat with a pair of tongs and slide the thermometer into the meat horizontally. You will get an instant reading. Once the chop or steak is removed from the pan, it will continue to cook and increase another 5°.

Pan sautéed Veal, Pork, Lamb, or Beef

1. Brush the marinade all over the chop. Ideally, this was done ahead of time for maximum effect.

2. Heat the sauté pan over medium-high heat for 1 minute.

3. Away from the flame, spray the sauté pan with a thin coat of non-stick spray.

4. Add the chop to the pan, and cook until both sides are well browned and the desired internal temperature is achieved. If the fat in the pan burns, it will spoil the deglazing. To avoid burning, adjust the heat to sear the meat but not burn the pan.

5. Once the meat is done, put it on a warm plate and lightly cover with foil. Rest the plate in a warm place.

6. Pour off any accumulated fat in the pan. Deglaze the pan with 1/2 cup of some combination of the following liquids: water, white wine or vermouth, chicken or beef stock. Add the liquid to the pan and scrape all the accumulated bits into the liquid. A teaspoon of balsamic vinegar may also be added. Reduce the volume by one half.

Ingredients

1 eight-ounce portion veal, pork, or lamb-chop, filet or steak.

2 teaspoons marinade (pp.44-45)

139

The sauce is now ready to pour over the chop. However you might want to add some of the following building blocks to the sauce after deglazing, to make it even more delicious:

Garlic. Add 1-2 teaspoons of roasted garlic purée.(p.19)

Mushrooms. Add $^1/_4$ cup of mushroom building block. (pp. 27-29)

Peppers. Add $^1/_4$ cup of chopped or puréed pepper. (p. 24)

Onions, leeks or shallots. Add $^1/_2$ cup of any of them to the sauce. (pp. 20-23)

Tomato. Either the concasse or oven dried tomato building block works well. (pp. 11-16)

Porcini mushroom essence is also a great flavor enhancer. (p. 30)

Mustard. If you like mustard, $^1/_2$ teaspoon may be added. Garlic with mustard is probably the most interesting choice.

Sherry or dry **marsala** wine may be used in the deglazing liquid.

Chopped Italian parsley, chives, basil, tarragon, or chervil dusted over the sauce will add the finishing touch to the dish.

To serve, just pour the sauce over the meat, or pour the sauce on the plate and set the meat on it.

Veal and Pork Scallops

Scallops are thin slices of meat usually cut from the leg of the veal or tenderloin of pork. The cooking method for scallops is slightly different than for chops and steaks, but the finishing touches with building blocks are similar.

The following recipe may be expanded according to the number of servings desired, allowing 5 ounces meat per person.

1. Flatten the scallops to a thickness of $^1/_8$ inch to prevent their curling when cooked. Make four $^1/_2$-inch cuts in the perimeter of the scallop.

2. In a sauté pan pour marinade and a little olive oil to just film the pan. Place over a medium-hot flame.

3. Dredge the scallops in flour, shaking off any excess.

4. Sauté the scallops quickly, one minute per side. Remove to a plate and keep warm.

5. Pour off any accumulated fat in the pan. Deglaze the pan with $^1/_2$ cup of the deglazing liquid and the balsamic vinegar.

Ingredients

5 ounces veal or pork scallops

$^1/_8$ cup flour, seasoned with $^1/_2$ teaspoon each of salt and pepper

2 teaspoons marinade (p.44)

extra olive oil

$^1/_2$ cup deglazing liquid—some combination of the following: water, white wine, dry vermouth, chicken or veal stock, mushroom essence. Dry Marsala wine is another classic deglazing option. Be sure to use a good quality Italian Marsala

$^1/_2$ - 1 teaspoon balsamic vinegar(optional)

6. Scrape all the accumulated particles off the surface of the pan to join the deglazing liquid. A flat spatula is a good choice for this task.

7. Return the scallops to the pan and simmer for one minute. Taste the sauce and adjust the salt and pepper.

You may make this recipe even more delicious with the addition of one or more of the following:

Garlic. Add ½ - 1 tablespoon sautéed or roasted garlic building block to the deglazing liquid. This makes a garlic-rich sauce. (p. 19)

Leeks. Adding ¼ – ½ cup of leek building block to the liquid will lend the leeks' creamy texture and flavor to the sauce. (p. 22)

Caramelized Onion. Add ¼ – ½ cup to the liquid. A teaspoon of balsamic vinegar will enhance the natural sweetness of the onions. (p. 21)

Roasted Pepper. Add ¼ – ½ cup of chopped pepper or pepper purée to the liquid. Pepper nectar maybe used as part of the deglazing liquid. A tablespoon of dry sherry is a nice addition. Just add to the deglazing liquid. A tablespoon of roasted garlic purée and a few tablespoons of onion, leek or shallot building block will make this even better. (p. 24)

Mushrooms. Add ¼ – ½ cup of one of the mushroom building blocks to the liquid. Here is the perfect time to use porcini mushroom essence in the liquid portion. Use a ratio of ⅓ essence to ⅔ stock/wine/water. The addition of garlic and onion building block will enhance the flavors. A few tablespoons of rough-chopped pepper will add flavor and visual appeal. (p. 28-31)

Tomato. Any of the tomato building blocks will work well here. Add ¼ – ½ cup to the liquid. Add a little oregano. In addition, a tablespoon of garlic, and onion, leek or shallot will add sweetness and flavor. Mushroom and pepper may also be added to make a more complex sauce. (p. 11-16)

For some heat, add a teaspoon of **red pepper flakes**. For a bit of extra zip, grate some **orange** or **lemon rind** into the deglazing liquid. A tablespoon or so of fresh-squeezed **orange** or **lemon juice** would be good. Only fresh-squeezed need apply. If using, reduce the liquid by half.

Cream or Crème Fraîche. You may add 1-2 tablespoons of cream or crème fraîche, if calories are not a problem. This will make for a very rich, creamy sauce.

Tart Shells, Dessert Building Blocks, and Desserts

A homemade dessert is the crown jewel of a fabulous meal.

Tart Shells

It's simple to make your own tart shells and freeze them. Avoid the raw, pre-made tart shells that are readily available in the frozen food section of the market. Their taste and texture leave much to be desired. With homemade tart shells in your freezer, quiches and tarts can be quickly assembled on short notice. Always use fresh, sweet butter, if possible, for the best taste and texture. Two types of tart shells, both from France, make the tastiest tarts easily: the classic pâte brisée, which is similar to American style pie dough, and sweet tart dough.

Pâte Brisée

See full recipe in Savoury Custards, Tarts, & Flans chapter, p.114.

Sweet Tart Dough

We have my good friend Carole Eiserloh of San Francisco to thank for this recipe. She gave me the original more than 20 years ago, and I have carried it around the world, baking a trail of tarts in my wake ever since. This is truly a no-fail dough, and no rolling is required!

While the basic dough is delicious, adding ground nuts to the recipe will add flavor and texture. Any of the following nuts—almonds, walnuts, pecans, hazelnuts, macadamia nuts, pine nuts, or pistachio—will work well. Sesame or poppy seeds may also be used. Add one half cup of ground nuts or whole seeds to the basic recipe. (See "notes on nuts," p.144).

1. Mix all ingredients together—either by hand, in a mixer, or in a food processor—until they are well blended and smooth. If using a food processor, pulse the nuts in after dough is smooth.

2. Scrape onto a sheet of plastic wrap. Wrap and shape into a brick.

3. Chill until firm.

4. To form the tart crust, slice the tart dough 1/8-inch thick and press into place. Leave the dough 1/8-inch above the rim. This will compensate for the slight shrinkage during the pre-baking. For easy removal it's best to grease the

Sweet Tart Dough Ingredients

½ cup sweet butter

¼ cup granulated sugar

1 cup regular flour

1 egg yolk

1 teaspoon pure vanilla extract

½ teaspoon pure almond extract (see Notes on Extracts, p.144)

pan first. The best way I have found to do this is to place the tart pan into the freezer for 15 minutes. Then spray or brush a coat of oil or melted butter on the pan. It will adhere better to the frozen surface.

5. Cover the bottom and sides of the pan, pushing with the balls of your fingers in quick movements. The less the dough is handled, the better. The goal is to place an even layer of dough in the pan.

6. Now, cover the surface with a sheet of plastic wrap. Press it lightly to cover the surface of the dough snugly.

7. Place in the freezer for at least one half hour to make the dough very firm. To achieve the best results, pre-bake the tart shell before adding the filling. Freezing helps the shell keep its shape during this initial baking.

Notes on Nuts

I like to grind nuts to a medium-fine consistency in a food processor. A wonderful trick is to freeze the nuts first and then grind them with the flour and sugar in the recipe. This prevents their oil from being released.

Nuts are full of oil and, like liquid oil, will become stale or rancid from exposure to heat. So the freezer is the best place to store them. Keep them tightly wrapped in two double zipper-lock bags. Buy them in bulk with some friends and have a selection in your freezer, ready to be used.

Notes on Extracts

Nothing is more vile than artificial vanilla extract. The perfume of pure vanilla is one of nature's most wonderful gifts—there is no substitute! While the standard supermarket vanilla extracts are passable, I recommend you invest in a bottle of well-made extract. They are available in specialty food stores and in food catalogues, such as Williams-Sonoma or King Arthur's flour.

I love to use **whole vanilla bean pods** in recipes calling for vanilla extract. They are easy to use: split a bean lengthwise and gently scrape the seeds out with a paring knife. Add to the other ingredients. Now put the vanilla bean in a jar and fill with sugar. The sugar will take on the perfume of the bean. Voilà–vanilla sugar!

Frangipane

A simple combination of basic ingredients from every baker's pantry will produce one of the most useful and delicious building blocks for pastry: *frangipane* (pronounced FRAN-juh-pan). Invented, according to the *Larousse Gastronomique*, by an Italian named Frangipani in the court of Louis XIII, frangipane has evolved into many recipes, but most include flour, sugar, eggs, butter, almonds, and vanilla. Quickly assembled with a food processor, frangipane may be prepared in advance and kept in the refrigerator for a week, or frozen for six months, to be pulled out just when you need to assemble a quick and tasty dessert. Using a chef's poetic license I have concocted several variations on frangipane with hazelnuts, walnuts, pecans, pistachios, or pinenuts.

Baked to a golden turn, frangipane has perfume, flavor, and a chewy texture that delight the palate. By combining frangipane with fresh fruit and fruit glazes, you can quickly and easily create unique and intensely flavored desserts. Among my favorites are *"Fig Jewels Set in Hazelnut-Lemon Frangipane,"* *"Stained Glass Fruit in Almond-Pinenut Frangipane,"* *"Pears Vesuvius with Pistachio Lava,"* and *"Apples in Maple Walnut Chemises."*

Frangipane can be used as a tart filling, baked in a shallow dish, or draped over fruit "à la chemise" (like a "shirt"). If you are baking it in a shallow dish, pick one that will make a good presentation, if possible.

This section presents first the basic recipe for frangipane building block, followed by variations on that recipe. Then, the fruit desserts that use this building block are presented, followed by a section on how to make the glazes for those desserts.

Basic Frangipane Ingredients

2 cups unsalted, shelled, blanched almonds, lightly toasted*

1/2 cup white flour

1/2 cup granulated sugar

1/2 cup melted sweet butter

3 large eggs

1 teaspoon pure vanilla extract, or the seeds of one vanilla pod.

Basic Frangipane

For more flavor, the rind of one whole lemon or orange may be added to the frangipane. As always, carefully grind off only the yellow or orange zest of the fruit, avoiding the bitter white pith underneath. One tablespoon of a fruit brandy or liqueur will add another layer of flavor. As an example, when using the frangipane for the Pears Vesuvius, add Poir Willams, a.k.a. pear brandy, Kirsch (cherry), Framboise (raspberry), Mirabelle (plum), or Grand Marnier (orange)—all are wonderful additions. Trimbach makes fine fruit brandy in half bottles. Avoid cut-rate brandies as they are a waste of money.

1. In a food processor, pulse-chop the nuts, flour, and sugar until the mixture resembles bread crumbs. Add the grated rinds of lemon or orange, if including them.

2. Add the melted butter and eggs to the food processor. Process at full speed until a smooth paste has formed. Scrape down the bowl once or twice during this process. The frangipane mixture is now complete.

You can store the frangipane in the refrigerator or freezer for later use.

> * lightly toasting nuts brings out their flavor. Because the frangipane will be baked, do not over-roast the nuts. Five minutes at 350˚ is about right. Hazelnuts, walnuts, and pistachios should be rubbed in a dish towel after roasting to remove the outer skin. Any of the nuts mentioned may be substituted for the almonds or used in combination.

All the following fruit desserts are best when the fruits are at their peak of ripeness. The best way to determine this is to use your nose. If you don't smell the perfume of the fruit, it won't have a good flavor. The following desserts may be made in advance and refrigerated. However, they will never be more delicious than when they have been out of the oven for 1 or 2 hours.

Fig Jewels in Hazelnut Frangipane

Is there anything more perfect than a ripe fig?

1. Preheat the oven to 350°.
2. Pre-bake the tart shell according to the recipe, or spray the flat dish with a non-stick spray.
3. Fill the tart/dish with the frangipane ⅔ full.
4. Set the figs into the frangipane, gently pushing them in. Arrange them in an interesting pattern.
5. Bake until the frangipane is golden brown. If the crust is browning before the frangipane, lightly spray a sheet of foil with a non-stick spray and gently drape the foil over the tart.
6. Remove from the oven and allow to cool.
7. When cool, brush the surface with the Passion Fruit/ Apricot Glaze.

Ingredients

12 ripe, fresh figs, washed, dried, and cut in half lengthwise

1 batch of hazelnut frangipane (p.146), with lemon rind and kirsch added

1 tart shell (p.143) or flat baking dish

1 batch of passion fruit/ apricot fruit glaze (recipe p.151)

Stained Glass Tart Ingredients

1 **Pre-baked tart shell (p.143) or flat baking pan**

Almond frangipane with ¹/₂ cup whole pine nuts folded in, made with orange rind and Grand Marnier (optional)

Raspberries

Blueberries

Apricots

Peaches

Mango

Apricot Grand Marnier Glaze (Recipes and techniques follow, p.151)

"Stained Glass" Tart

This tart uses a variety of fresh fruits set in a beautiful pattern. When glazed, it looks like a stained glass window!

1. Preheat the oven to 350°.
2. Prepare the fruit. Remember all fruit should be as dry as possible.
- **Raspberries and blueberries:** lightly rinse, remove any stems, and blot dry on paper towels.
- **Apricots and Peaches:** wash, dry, remove pit and cut into crescents.
- **Mangoes:** peel and cut into crescent shapes.
3. Fill the tart shell or baking dish ²/₃ full with frangipane.
4. Arrange the fruit in an interesting pattern, contrasting the shapes and colors on the surface of the frangipane.
5. Bake as for the fig tart, covering with foil if crust is browning before the frangipane is done.
6. Remove from oven and allow to cool.
7. Glaze with the Apricot Grand Marnier Glaze.

Pears Vesuvius with Pistachio Almond "Lava"

The poet Frank Lima named this dessert when we presented it at a dinner party for Bill de Kooning in East Hampton in the early '80s.

1. Squeeze the lemon and strain the juice to remove pits. Pour into a non-aluminum bowl large enough to hold the pears.

2. Peel the pears: hold the bottom end in your palm. With a vegetable peeler, cut down in a straight line, starting at the stem end and continuing to the bottom end. Turn and repeat until all the skin has been removed. This method will keep the pears' natural shape intact. As you finish peeling each pear, gently roll it in the lemon juice. This will prevent discoloring and add flavor.

3. With a melon baller, scoop out the core of each pear, starting at the bottom end and boring a tunnel clear through the stem end. Trim just enough of the pear bottom so it will sit up straight. Line a cookie sheet or baking dish with parchment paper, and spray it with a non-stick spray. Place the pears 2-inches apart. Save the lemon juice for the glaze.

4. Spoon the frangipane over the pear. The goal is to have the frangipane coat the sides of the pear and the hole in the middle. This creates the "lava flow."

5. Bake in a 350° oven until the pear is tender and the frangipane is golden brown—approximately 45 minutes. Test the pears with a toothpick on the inside of the hole, so as not to damage the outside. A toothpick should easily pierce the flesh. If the pears are still hard and the frangipane is already golden brown, take a piece of aluminum foil, spray with non-stick spray, and gently drape over the pears. Our goal is to bake until the pears are tender, but if you overbake, the volcano will collapse. This will not affect the taste, but will not be as interesting a presentation. Allow the pears to cool.

6. Glaze with the orange glaze.

7. Dust with finely chopped pistachio nuts.

Ingredients

6 ripe pears

1 lemon

1 recipe Pistachio-almond frangipane (p.146), made with a 50-50 mix of each nut, and with orange rind and Kirsch

2 tablespoons chopped pistachios for garnish

Orange Glaze (next section, p.152)

149

Apples in Maple Walnut Chemises

Ingredients

6 tart apples, like Granny Smith

1 lemon

1 recipe for Walnut Frangipane (p.146) made with lemon rind and framboise

Raspberry Glaze (see next section, p.152)

1. Preheat the oven to 350°.

2. Squeeze the lemon and strain to remove any pits.

3. Peel the apples. To keep the apples' round shape, peel in circles parallel to the "equator" of the apple.

4. Using a melon baller, dig out the core from top to bottom.

5. Toss the apples in lemon juice coating, inside and out.

6. Slice off just enough of the bottom so the apple sits flat.

7. Line a cookie sheet or baking dish with parchment paper, and spray it with a non-stick spray. Place the apples 2 inches apart. Save the lemon juice for the glaze.

8. Spoon the walnut frangipane over the apples to completely cover them, like a shirt.

9. Bake until the frangipane is golden and the apples are tender. The same principle applies here as for the pears: cook until tender, but not until they collapse!

10. Glaze with the raspberry glaze.

Fruit Glazes

Fruit glazes are easy to make. Seek out good quality jellies and jams with the fruit listed as the first ingredient. To these, add lemon juice, which cuts the cloying sweetness of the jam, and liqueur (always optional), which adds a depth of flavor. If you are working with fruit that was in a lemon juice bath, by all means use the strained juice in the glaze.

Glaze should always be applied to a cooled surface and used very hot. This will allow the glaze to be applied smoothly and evenly. Use a natural fiber brush to apply the glaze. I like to keep a brush on hand for just this purpose. Dip one-inch of the brush into the glaze and gently brush the surface of the tart or fruit. Be alert for brush bristles that may come loose during the "painting" process. Carefully pick them off.

Apricot Glaze

1. Put all ingredients in a small sauce pan.
2. Bring to a boil over a medium flame, stirring gently. Reduce to a simmer and cook 5 minutes.
3. Strain into a small bowl.
4. The glaze is ready to use.

It's handy to use a microwaveable bowl to make reheating easy. Remember to reheat gently to prevent the glaze from boiling over. Handle glaze with care.

Ingredients

2 cups apricot jam

¹/₄ cup fresh-squeezed lemon juice

2-3 tablespoons Grand Marnier, Cointreau, Kirsch, or Mirabelle (optional)

Apricot / Passion Fruit Glaze.

For a more exotic flavor add the pulp from 2 passion fruits to the jam before cooking. Follow recipe above.

Passion Fruit Glaze

Passion fruit jelly, though hard to find, makes a super glaze. Follow the same recipe as for apricot glaze, but omit the liqueur. The trick is to find the passion fruit jelly. The wonderful Paris-based shop Hediard makes a super passion fruit jelly. If you are in Paris, do stop by the shop on Place de la Madeleine and stock up. What a wonderful excuse for a trip to Paris! Dean & DeLuca in New York City is another possible source. A combination of apricot and passion fruit jams works very well also.

Raspberry or Red Current Glaze Ingredients

- 2 cups seedless raspberry jam (Triptree makes a fine seedless jam) or red current jam
- 1/4 cup lemon juice
- 2-3 tablespoons framboise or kirsch liqueur

Raspberry or Red Current Glaze

1. Combine all the ingredients together in a small saucepan and bring to a boil over a medium flame. Reduce and simmer 5 minutes.
2. Strain. It's ready to use.

Orange or Lemon Glaze Ingredients

- 2 cups orange or lemon marmalade, or a combination of the two
- 1/4 cup lemon juice
- 3 tablespoons Grand Marnier or other orange based liqueur

Orange or Lemon Glaze

1. Process as for apricot glaze (p.151).

While these are the glazes I make and use most often, almost any fruit jam will make a glaze. Always add lemon juice and strain for the best results.

Simple Sponge Cake

I have made this cake so often, I think I could do it in my sleep. It is really a no-fail cake. Just be careful not to over- or under-bake it. The recipe makes two cakes, but it's easy to halve the recipe for one. Before you begin, prepare your cake pan. Lightly grease by spraying with a non-stick spray, or brush with butter. Place a piece of parchment paper, cut to fit snugly, on the bottom of the pan. Spray or brush again with butter or oil, then lightly dust with flour. Tap out excess flour.

1. Crack eggs into a bowl, being careful to avoid any bits of eggshells. Remember, the easy way to remove a stray bit of shell is with a larger piece of shell.

2. Add one cup of sugar.

3. Place the bowl over a pot of simmering water and whisk until warm to the touch. This will help the eggs whip up to a large volume. If you are in any doubt as to whether you have any eggshells in the mix, pour through a strainer.

4. Beat until batter is quite thick. This should take about 8 minutes with a hand-held beater, or 5 minutes in a Hobart-type mixer.

5. Now, gradually sift the flour over the mixture and fold into the mixture with a spatula or whisk. Working quickly, cut and fold to deflate the egg mixture as little as possible.

6. Fold in the vanilla extract.

7. Scrape into the prepared pan. Tap the pan gently to set the batter. Take a spatula and gently swirl a slight depression in the center of the batter. This will help compensate for the natural tendency of the cake to rise more in the center of the pan, resulting in a more even cake.

8. Bake in a preheated 350° oven on a rack in the center of the oven until the cake has risen and turned a golden brown. It should shrink slightly from the sides of the pan, and a skewer or toothpick should come out free from batter when inserted into the center of the cake, the last part to finish baking. The baking time will depend on the size of the cake pan. If you are using two 9 or 10-inch pans, the cakes should be done in about 15 minutes. If you are using a larger, single pan, 12-14-inches, it will take about 20 min-

Ingredients

6 eggs

1 cup sugar

1 cup flour, sifted with 1 additional tablespoon sugar

1 teaspoon high quality vanilla extract

153

utes. The cake may also be baked in a sheet pan. This will be the quickest to cook—about 7-8 minutes.

If you want to make a roulade, or rolled cake, roll the cake while it's still warm. Loosen the parchment paper from the bottom of the pan and roll so the paper remains attached to the cake. Cloth-lined rubber gloves make for happy, non-burnt fingers. Remember all ovens are different, so take a peek after $3/4$ of the time has elapsed to see how the cake looks.

Remove cake from the oven and set on a wire rack to cool.

The cake is ready to eat—simple but tasty. One way to enhance the flavor is to brush it with a simple sugar syrup, flavored with your favorite liqueur, vanilla beans, or both! Another is to split the cake and fill with fresh fruit, a fruit glaze, or fresh fruit sauce. Freshly made whipped cream adds a heavenly touch, as do ice cream or sorbet. Recipes follow.

If using roulade, unroll, peel off paper, and proceed as above.

The cakes, well wrapped, will keep frozen a few months.

Ingredients

1 cup granulated sugar

1 cup water

$1/4$ cup of your favorite liqueur. Good choices include Grand Marnier, Cognac, and any of the fruit brandies like kirsch or framboise.

1 vanilla bean, split (may be used alone or in combination with the liqueurs)

Simple Sugar Syrup

1. Add all the ingredients to a small saucepan.
2. Bring to a boil and simmer 5 minutes or until all the sugar has dissolved.
3. Cool, leaving the vanilla bean in the syrup.
4. It's ready to use and may be stored in a covered jar in the refrigerator.

To use the syrup, dip a pastry brush into the syrup and brush over the surface of the cake. You may want to split the cake in two, slicing across the equator to make 2 even disks, so you can have more surface to brush with sugar syrup. Remember that the surface of the cake that rested on the bottom of the pan will be the smoothest surface. If you are not splitting the cake, poke holes across the surface with a skewer to allow the syrup to penetrate into the cake.

Fruit glazes

Any of the fruit glazes (p.151) will add extra flavor and a nice sheen to the cake. Preserves also work well, but give them the same treatment as our glazes, without the straining step, to make them much more flavorful. I like to dust the surface with chopped, toasted nuts.

Whipped Cream

Making whipped cream is simple, but remember that the bowl and beater should be cold for the best results. Most recipes call for sugar to be added to the cream. When using the cream with these cakes, I like to whip it sugar-free but with vanilla bean seeds or extract added. With the sugar syrup, the cakes are very sweet and the unsweetened cream makes a nice counterpoint.

There is a product I love called "Whip It", made by Oetker. It's a powder stabilizer that makes the cream stiff and easy to spread. If you can find it, by all means use it.

Ingredients

1 pint heavy cream

1 vanilla bean, split and seeded (p.144) or 1 teaspoon vanilla extract

2 packs Whip It (optional)

1. Place beater and bowl in the freezer for one half hour
2. Pour cream into bowl, stir in the seeds from the vanilla pod, or stir in the extract.
3. Mix in the Whip It, if using.
4. Beat until the cream holds stiff peaks.

Ice Cream or Sorbet Cake

1. Remove ice cream/sorbet from freezer and allow to soften just enough to be malleable.
2. Split cake, and brush with syrup. (always optional)
3. Line the pan the cake was baked in with plastic wrap, leaving 4-inches of wrap above the rim.
4. Place the bottom layer, baked side down, in pan. Add a layer of ice cream or sorbet. Place the top layer on cake and either add another layer of ice cream/sorbet or leave uncovered. If leaving uncovered, cover with fruit glaze and a dusting of toasted nuts.
5. Pull plastic wrap up and press across the top of the cake.
6. Freeze for at least 2 hours before serving.

Fresh Fruit Sauces

When fruit is ripe and inexpensive, take advantage and make fruit sauces. Poured over ice cream, sorbet, tarts, or cakes, fruit sauces add an extra special touch. Always smell the fruit for its perfume. Remember: no perfume, no flavor.

Fruit sauces can be made from any fruit. Berries, especially raspberries and blackberries, are the ones that get me most excited.

All fruit sauces freeze very well.

Ingredients

- 1 pint fresh raspberries/blackberries (any combination of the two or solo)
- ¼ cup raspberry or blackberry preserves
- 1 teaspoon vanilla extract or ½ vanilla bean, split and seeded (p.144)

Fresh Raspberry or Blackberry Sauce

This recipe makes a rich, flavorful sauce. I sometimes add strawberries and blueberries. But I think nothing is more intense and delicious than a pure raspberry sauce.

1. Place the berries and preserves in a microwaveable dish. Microwave for 5 minutes. Alternatively, heat together in a saucepan until preserves are melted and the berries soft—about 5 minutes.

2. Press the berries through a strainer with fine holes, rubbing the fruit mixture against the sides with a rubber spatula to extract the fruit pulp and juice.

3. Keep pressing until all that remains are the berry seeds.

4. Stir in the vanilla extract or vanilla seeds.

Fresh Apricot, Peach, or Mango Sauce

Any of these fruits can be made into a sauce in the same way. Use separately or in combination.

1. Wash fruit. Drain.
2. Remove the pits from the apricots and peaches. Peel and section the mango.
3. Combine the fruit, preserves, and vanilla bean in a sauté pan.
4. Over medium heat, cook until jam melts. Simmer fruit for 10 minutes.
5. Place in food processor and purée. Add vanilla extract, if using.
6. Press through a fine strainer to produce a smooth sauce.

Variations

Passion fruit adds a wonderful flavor and perfume. Add the pulp of 2-3 passion fruits, or use passion fruit jam in place of the other preserves.

Ingredients

1 pound very ripe fruit—any combination of apricots, peaches, and mangoes

1/2 cup apricot, peach, or mango preserves

2 teaspoons lemon juice

1 teaspoon vanilla extract or 1/2 vanilla bean pod (p.144)

Frozen Fruit Purée

With fruit sauce in the freezer, frozen fruit purée—a cross between sorbet and granita, only better—is just a food processor whirl away! Both sorbet and granita use a base of sugar syrup along with the fruit sauce. Using the fruit sauce we've made, the only added sugar is the preserves. It makes an intense, fruity dessert.

1. Chill bowl and blade of food processor in the freezer for 1/2 hour.
2. Break or cut the frozen fruit sauce into 1-inch square cubes. If the sauce was frozen flat in zipper-lock bags, this is a snap (literally)!
3. Add sauce to the bowl of the food processor and pulse until sauce is processed into a slush.
4. Spoon into a wineglass and serve. Pre-chilling the glasses in the freezer is a good idea.
5. For an extra special treat, layer with whipped cream and add toasted nuts. Toasted nuts may be added to the slush in the food processor. The nuts should be toasted, rough chopped, and very cold before adding to the fruit sauce cubes.

Caramel, Caramel Chocolate, and Chocolate Sauces

These sauces are easy to make. You can keep any of these sauces frozen until you are ready to spoon it over your favorite dessert.

Caramel Sauce

Ingredients

1 cup granular white sugar

½ cup water

1 teaspoon strained, fresh-squeezed lemon juice. *We strain the lemon juice to remove the pits and the pulp.*

½ cup heavy cream.

If possible, try to use cream that hasn't been 'ultra-pasteurized,' it's sweeter and tastier—hard to find, but worth seeking out.

1 tablespoon sweet butter

1 teaspoon best quality vanilla extract or the scraped seeds from one vanilla bean (p.144)

1. Combine the sugar, water, and strained lemon juice into a one quart sauce pan. Stir until the sugar is the consistency of wet sand. Take a clean pastry brush, dip it in cold water, and brush down the sides of the pan to wash off any sugar clinging to the sides of the pan.

2. Place over medium-high heat and cover. Cook for 5 minutes and uncover. The accumulated steam will wash down any remaining sugar crystals

3. Cook until the sugar is a deep, golden brown. Be careful once the sugar starts to turn brown—it cooks very rapidly.

4. When the desired color has been achieved, remove from heat and place cover over pan, leaving a gap to pour the cream through. Pour the cream into the hot mixture. It will sputter and pop!

5. Wait one minute, remove cover, and—over low heat—stir to dissolve the caramelized sugar. Stir until the sauce is smooth.

6. Stir in the butter and vanilla.

7. This sauce is very sweet, and it's now ready to use.

You can pour it into a squeeze-bottle, a.k.a. ketchup/mustard server. Use a funnel to make this an easier task. Now you are ready to drizzle the sauce all over the place! I like to keep a bottle in the freezer—45 seconds in the microwave and I'm doing my best Jackson Pollack number over the ice cream!

Chocolate Caramel Sauce

1. With a knife or in a food processor cut the chocolate into fine bits.
2. Stir into the warm caramel sauce to melt.
3. Stir in the liqueur, if using.

You may use and serve as for the caramel sauce.

Ingredients

1 recipe for caramel sauce (above)

4 ounces bitter chocolate (100% cocoa butter, no sugar). I use bitter chocolate because the caramel sauce is so sweet. Bitter chocolate makes it a bit less cloying. I recommend Valrhona or Scharffen Berger; both companies make divine bitter chocolate.

1-2 tablespoons Grand Mariner or your favorite liqueur (optional)

Chocolate Sauce

Stovetop method

1. In a saucepan combine the chocolate and the cream.
2. Over medium heat stir the cream and chocolate until chocolate is melted and the sauce smooth.
3. Stir in the liqueur, if using.

Microwave method

1. Combine the cream and chocolate in a microwave-compatible bowl.
2. Zap in 30 second increments at medium heat (power 5) for a total of 2 minutes.
3. Remove and stir. Return to microwave and repeat until the cream is warm and the chocolate melted.
4. Stir in the liqueur.

The **squeeze-bottle method** outlined for caramel sauce works very well here also.

Chocolate Sauce Ingredients

1/2 pint heavy cream

8 ounces bittersweet chocolate, cut into small pieces. I prefer Valrhona or Scharffen Berger.

1-2 tablespoons Grand Marnier or your favorite liqueur

Index

tomato orange risotto 102
tomato sauce 56
veal and pork scallops 140
vegetable stock 39
Vinaigrette
basic recipe 72
basil 73
caramelized onion 73
citrus 73
garlic 72
garlic-Parmesan 72
garlic-roasted pepper (1) 72
garlic-roasted pepper (2) 73
garlic-tomato 73
leek 73
red, white, sherry wine or balsamic
vinaigrette 72
salad dressings 71
vinaigrette with body 73
Vinegar
basil 48
bouquet garni 49
bean salad 65
caramelized onion spread 71
caramelized onion tart 119
chervil 49
chicken with caramelized onion 130
grilled fish filet 126
herb infused 48-49
herbs de Provence 49
hot pepper 49
marinade 45
melitzano salata 68
roasted pepper puree 70
salad dressings 71-73
salmon 124
sherry wine vinegar with garlic,
thyme, and bay leaf 49
skordalais 70
tarragon   49
veal and pork scallops 140
Walnuts
apples in walnut chemises 150
chicken mousse 137
frangipane 145-146
mushroom polenta 97
melitzano salata 68
pesto 62

polenta 96
skordaliais 70
sweet tart dough 143
toasting 62
Whipped cream 155
White truffle oil
mushroom in broth 88
mushroom risotto 100
mushroom pizza 111
White wine
beef stock 41
chicken garlic demi glace sauce 137
fish filet sauté 123
leek and shrimp 103
marinade 45
melitzano salata 68
mushroom risotto 100
pan sauté of veal, pork, lamb or beef 139
pepper sauce 61
risotto with red pepper 102
sauté of chicken breast or thigh 129
seafood tomato 59
shrimp with garlic sauce 121
veal and pork sauté 140
vegetable stock 39
whole French roasted chicken 131
Zipper locking bag 51

Printed in the United States
762200004B